Media Law in Sweden

Media Law in Sweden

Second Edition

Joakim Nergelius

This book was originally published as a monograph in the International Encyclopaedia of Laws/Media Law.

Founding Editor: Roger Blanpain†
General Editor: Frank Hendrickx
Volume Editors: Peggy Valcke & Eva Lievens

Wolters Kluwer

Published by:
Kluwer Law International B.V.
PO Box 316
2400 AH Alphen aan den Rijn
The Netherlands
E-mail: lrs-sales@wolterskluwer.com
Website: www.wolterskluwer.com/en/solutions/kluwerlawinternational

Sold and distributed by:
Wolters Kluwer Legal & Regulatory U.S.
920 Links Avenue
Landisville, PA 17538
United States of America
E-mail: customer.service@wolterskluwer.com

DISCLAIMER: The material in this volume is in the nature of general comment only. It is not offered as advice on any particular matter and should not be taken as such. The editor and the contributing authors expressly disclaim all liability to any person with regard to anything done or omitted to be done, and with respect to the consequences of anything done or omitted to be done wholly or partly in reliance upon the whole or any part of the contents of this volume. No reader should act or refrain from acting on the basis of any matter contained in this volume without first obtaining professional advice regarding the particular facts and circumstances at issue. Any and all opinions expressed herein are those of the particular author and are not necessarily those of the editor or publisher of this volume.

ISBN 978-94-035-6810-2

e-Book: ISBN 978-94-035-6820-1
web-PDF: ISBN 978-94-035-6830-0

The Author

Joakim Nergelius has been Professor of law at the University of Örebro, Sweden, since September 2003, as well as associate professor (docent) in European and Comparative Law at Abo Academy (*Turku*), Finland.

He has written extensively on Swedish, comparative and European Constitutional Law. Among his works are *Konstitutionellt rättighetsskydd – Svensk rätt i ett komparativt perspektiv* (Constitutional Protection of Human Rights – Swedish Law in a Comparative Perspective), *Stockholm (Norstedts) 1996* (doctoral dissertation). *Amsterdamfördraget och EU:s institutionella maktbalans* (The Treaty of Amsterdam and the Institutional Power Balance in the EU), *Stockholm (Norstedts; Institutet för rättsvetenskaplig forskning) 1998*,Svensk statsrätt (Lund, Studentlitteratur, 3rd ed 2014) and the anthology, *Nordic and Other European Constitutional Traditions, Brill/Nijhoff (Leiden/Boston) 2006*. More recently, he published the book *The Constitutional Dilemma of the European Union* in 2009 and the monograph Svensk statsrätt (5th ed 2022).

The Author

Table of Contents

Preface

After quite a long time 'in the making', the second edition of this monograph of Swedish Media Law is finally completed. It brings me great joy and satisfaction to present an updated version of this text on a topic which is of great constitutional importance in Sweden and at the same time quite technically complicated (which means that changes may sometimes occur quickly). However, I hope that the reader who has taken the time to study this rather complicated area, with few if any equivalents in other countries, will feel at least slightly enlightened, or perhaps 'confused at a higher level' when having digested it.

Malmö in September 2025
Joakim Nergelius

List of Abbreviations

A/S	Aktieselskab (Denmark, Norway)
COM	Commission (EU, in its own documents)
ECtHR	European Court of Human Rights
ECHR	European Convention of Human Rights
ECJ	European Court of Justice
ECR	European Court Reports
EU	European Union
FPA	Freedom of Press Act (Tryckfrihetsförordningen, TF)
FSA	Freedom of Speech Act (Yttrandefrihetsgrundlagen, YGL)
Hudoc	Human Rights Documentation (webpage of ECtHR)
IG	Instrument of Government (Regeringsformen, RF)
KU	Konstitutionsutskottet
MDA	Marknadsdomstolens avgöranden
MP, MPs	Member(s) of Parliament
NJA	Nytt Juridiskt Arkiv
OSL	Offentlighets- och sekretesslagen
Prop, prop	Proposition (law bill)
PuL	Personuppgiftslagen
RÅ	Regeringsrättens Årsbok
rskr	riksdagsskrivelse
SEK	Swedish currency (crowns)
SOU	Statens Offentliga utredningar

List of Abbreviations

General Introduction

§1. General Background of the Country

I. Political and Legal System of the Country

A. Introduction

1. The Swedish legal system is based, like most other legal systems in the world, on the idea of an existing hierarchy of norms. Still, that is not very clearly expressed in the Swedish Constitution, where it may only indirectly be deduced from the role of judicial review in Chapter 11, Article 14 of the Instrument of Government (IG), according to which courts or other public bodies may set aside provisions that are in conflict with rules of fundamental law 'or other superior statute'.

2. This provision, though until recently rarely used, would of course be meaningless without an existing hierarchy of norms. Nevertheless, that concept has in fact never been very clearly developed in Swedish Constitutional law, where it may even be said that the concept of the Constitution as *higher law* or *lex superior* was not very clear when the IG (which is by far the most important constitutional act) was enacted in 1974. At that time, a perspective highly inspired by popular sovereignty prevailed, according to which the constitution contains rules that describe the political situation and issues such as what should happen and which procedure is to be followed when the Prime Minister is appointed, or laws are enacted or, in other words, that the constitution is mainly and above all descriptive in its nature. The opposite and internationally more common view, based on the idea of *constitutionalism*, according to which the Constitution is the *higher law*, against which all other laws are to be measured and reviewed, has only quite recently, in the last fifteen or twenty years and in the light of the wholly new influence of European law, been seriously discussed. Undoubtedly, that new perspective is now gaining ground, which could be seen not least in the official, governmental instructions (direktiv 2004:96) to the parliamentary committee preparing a constitutional reform for 2010 (*Grundlagsutredningen*) as well as in the important constitutional changes enacted on 1 January 2011.[1]

1. In the doctrine, this tension between old and new ideas and perspectives, between popular sovereignty and constitutionalism in other words, is analysed in particular by Nergelius, Svensk statsrätt, in Ch. 1 and in the structure of the book, which is built around this distinction. *See also* my study on Swedish Constitutional Law in the IEL series (with a 4th edition in 2025). The main report from

3. The main trait or characteristic feature of the Swedish Constitution, identified here as IG, is its emphasis on popular sovereignty. According to its very first sentence, in Chapter 1, Article 1, section 1, 'All public power in Sweden proceeds from the people.' This, however, is not only a declaratory statement against the concept of separation of powers, but a viewpoint and an attitude that also influences other parts of the Swedish constitutional system.

4. One aspect of this principled approach, though perhaps not the most important one, is the relative ease with which the constitutions may be changed. According to Chapter 8, Article 14 IG, the constitutional acts or fundamental laws are enacted, changed or amended by means of two decisions of identical wording (*see also* Chapter 8, Articles 15 and 18). The second decision, however, may not be taken until elections for the Parliament have been held and the newly-elected parliament has been convened. At least nine months shall elapse between the day when the matter was first submitted to the Riksdag and the date of the election, unless the parliamentary committee on the constitution (*Konstitutionsutskottet, KU*) grants an exception from that provision by means of a decision supported by five-sixths of its members.[2] But it must be noted that a qualified majority of the 349 Member(s) of Parliaments (MPs) is not required on any of those occasions. Instead, a majority of the MPs present and voting is sufficient both times, which is surprising and even astonishing when seen in an international perspective.

5. A certain protection for parliamentary minorities is here provided by Chapter 8, Article 16 IG, which stipulates that a referendum shall be held on a proposal concerning fundamental law which is held in abeyance over an election, on a motion to this effect by at least one tenth of the MPs, provided that at least one third of them will concur in approving the motion.[3] The referendum will then be held simultaneously with the parliamentary election. The proposal is rejected if a majority of those taking part in the referendum vote against it and if the number of those voting against will exceed half the number of those who registered a valid vote in the general election.

6. Still, in an international perspective, it seems clear that the Swedish constitutional acts are unusually easy to change or amend, in particular when its rules are seen in connection with the fact that the highly technical nature of the Freedom of Press Act (FPA) and Freedom of Speech Act (FSA), which both contain huge sections of criminal, procedural and civil law, has led to a series of regular constitutional changes (in total more than 200) since 1974. When no constitutional

---

Grundlagsutredningen is SOU 2008:125, followed by the governmental bill 2009/10:80. For a recent comment in English, *see* Nergelius, Constitutional Reform in Sweden: Some Important Remarks, Tijdschrift voor Constitutioneel Recht (Netherlands) 2013 pp. 372–379.

2. In s. 2 of the same article, it is also stated that The Riksdag may not adopt as a decision held in abeyance over an election a proposal for the enactment of fundamental law which conflicts with any other proposal concerning fundamental law currently being held in abeyance, unless at the same time it rejects the proposal it first adopted.
3. Such a motion must be put forward within fifteen days from the date on which the Riksdag adopted the proposal which is to be held in abeyance.

amendments were proposed for the election in 2006, it was the first and only time since 1974 that this had happened! It should also be noted that the possibility for a referendum on a proposed constitutional amendment, which should in its result be legally and constitutional binding, has so far never been used.

7. From a political point of view, however, those rules are best understood from the aspect that they contribute to consensus concerning constitutional changes among the main political parties, notably the social democrats and the right-wing parties. In fact, politically disputed or contested constitutional amendments have so far been extremely unusual, a fact that has, in a way, until now diminished the practical importance and consequences of the fact that the constitutional acts are so relatively easy to change or amend, when seen in an international perspective.

8. According to Chapter 1, Article 4, section 1 of the IG, the Parliament or *Riksdag* is the foremost representative of the people. It is thus logical, given the emphasis on popular sovereignty that is so characteristic of the Swedish Constitution, that legislation is a dominant source of law and that it is easy to pass.

9. The main rule on how legislation is passed is to be found in Chapter 4, Article 7 IG, which states that when a vote is taken in the Parliament, the opinion in which more than half of those voting concur will constitute its decision. Legislation is of course included here, without being expressly mentioned. There are certain rules on requirements for a qualified majority, in certain exceptional situations, to be found both in the IG and the special Riksdag Act, but these are highly irregular and very rarely used.

B. *Form of Government*

1. Central Authorities of the State

10. Sweden is a parliamentary democracy based on popular sovereignty and rule of law at the same time, as follows from Chapter 1, Article 1 of the IG, the Constitution of 1974. The independence of the respective executive, legislative and judicial powers is guaranteed through various provisions of the Constitution, but the idea of separation of powers was not present when the new Constitution, replacing an ancient and partly even obsolete constitution from 1809, was elaborated in the 1960s and 1970s.

11. The Parliament (*Riksdag*, *riksdagen*) consists of 349 members, all sitting in the same chamber. National elections take place every four years in September and, at the same time, municipal elections take place to the 285 municipalities. (However, in 2010, the possibility to organize municipal elections between the parliamentary elections was introduced.) The election system is strictly proportional. Each party which gains at least 4% of the votes in the country will be represented in Parliament. At the moment (September 2025), eight parties are represented there.

12. Ever since the unicameral parliament was introduced in 1970, elections to three levels of political decision-making, i.e., Parliament, county councils or regions and municipalities have been held simultaneously, which means that they were held on the third Sunday of September, originally every third year but since 1994 every fourth year. In 2014, the election day was changed to the second Sunday of September. This manner of organizing the election procedure is far from the only one possible, but a number of committees – the latest one in 2002[4] – have argued against introducing separate election days for local and national elections, mainly because it might lead to a lower electoral turnout in the local elections.[5]

13. Here, two interesting changes appeared in 2010, in the shape of a possibility for the municipalities to organize separate elections between the regular elections every fourth year – which will however not free them from the obligation to organize new, regular ones 'next time around', so to speak – and that the elections have been moved to the second Sunday as of September in 2014.

14. If we focus on the national elections, we may note that the Parliament is, according to Chapter 3, Article 1 IG appointed by means of free, secret and direct elections. Voting in such elections is by party, with an option for the voter to express a preference for a particular candidate. The fact that those elections are 'free' does of course mean that each voter gives his vote freely to the party that he or she finds best, having – hopefully – studied their respective programmes carefully. The secrecy refers to the fact that the voter does not have to reveal how he votes, which corresponds to the right guaranteed by Chapter 2, Article 2 IG of not having to reveal one's political opinion. At election time, the voter may pick as many party lists as he wishes, but once in the electoral booth, he may only put one into each envelope (one for each election). Should he or she wish to openly declare his preference for a certain party, that is of course also allowed.

15. According to Chapter 3, Article 4 IG, every Swedish citizen who is currently or who has ever been domiciled within the Realm is entitled to vote in the Parliamentary election, given that he or she has attained the age of 18 on or before the election day. The rule seems old-fashioned from the point of view that it is today quite easy to imagine a Swedish citizen who has never been domiciled within the Realm, in which case it is hard to justify why that person should not be entitled to vote. Difficult cases are to be decided on the basis of an electoral roll drawn up before the election; the more detailed rules concerning that roll are to be found in the Electoral Law (*Vallagen*).[6] The same criteria apply in order to be elected as an MP, according to IG Chapter 3, Article 4, section 3.

---

4. *See* the official report SOU 2002:42, Den gemensamma valdagen och andra valfrågor.
5. There is undoubtedly a political reality behind this commitment to a procedure decided in the 1970s, namely that the Social Democrats fear losing influence in many municipalities if the elections to those would take place independently of the national elections, during which the Social Democratic Party, traditionally and historically an unusually effective political power-machine, may use its whole 'artillery' and resources also to influence the outcome of the local elections.
6. *See* in particular Ch. 7, Art. 1 of that law.

16. Thus, a one-chamber system, which is closely related to the proportional electoral system, has existed since 1970. The historical background to this is that the right-wing parties were in favour of such a reform ever since 1945. Having faced a setback in the local elections of 1966, when the issue suddenly became important, the Social Democrats accepted to change their position on the issue, though the proportional system and the simultaneous election day as well as the role of the Monarchy were then also parts of the 'package' or reform. The sudden need for this reform may today seem slightly surprising, since the period of the bicameral legislature, 1866–1970, was historically extremely successful for Sweden. But sometimes political changes are not entirely logical as for the way in which they happen.

17. Anyway, as mentioned *above,* the electoral system is based on the division of the Realm into specific constituencies for the parliamentary elections. According to Chapter 3, Article 6 IG, the Riksdag comprises 310 fixed constituency seats and 39 adjustment seats. While the fixed constituency seats are distributed among the constituencies on the basis of a calculation of the relationship between the number of persons entitled to vote in each constituency and the total number of persons entitled to vote throughout the whole of the Realm, which will always be beneficial for the main, biggest parties, the function and idea of the 39 adjustment seats may be said to be to compensate the smaller parties for their 'losses' there, in relation to their total numbers of votes throughout the whole country (*see* Chapter 3, Article 8 for more details).

18. As follows from Chapter 3, Article 7, only parties who have received at least 4% of the votes cast throughout the whole country are entitled to take a share in the distribution of seats. Since the system is proportional, a party that has for instance won 5% of the votes shall also get 5% of the seats. One exception may lead to deviations – though it has so far never happened – namely if a party should win at least 12% of the votes in one particular constituency, but less than 4% in the country as a whole. Apart from that possibility, however, the system is 'working' from the point of view that it really leads to the effects wished for in terms of proportionality and, thus, a fair result. On the other hand, it is clear that it does not facilitate the birth of strong governments, possessing a strong majority in the Parliament. When a majority government entered into power in October 2006, supported by 178 MPs, this was actually the first time since May 1981 that such a government ruled. However, after October 2010 (and again after the election in 2014 until September 2022), Sweden was led by a minority government. After the election in 2022, the three-party right-wing minority government enjoys majority in the Parliament thanks to support from the far-right Swedish Democrats (whose programme against migration and criminality has, as a compensation for the support, become official Swedish policy).

19. According to Chapter 3, Article 1 IG, the voting in the elections is by party, with an option for the voter to express a preference for a particular candidate. So far, however, that latter possibility, which was introduced in 1998, has not had any big importance. It is possible that it would grow more important should the possibility of extraordinary elections be wider. So far, extraordinary elections have surprisingly enough never taken place in Sweden, which may be due to the fact that if they should occur, the ordinary election will take place as planned anyway (*see* Chapter 3, Articles 3–4 in combination).[7] In the directives to the committee preparing a Constitutional reform, a change of this rule was envisaged, which could perhaps have meant that, should an extraordinary election take place, the new ordinary election should not take place within four years from the date of that election. It seems likely that such a move would have been able to vitalize the political climate of the country and the party system, in particular, since it would in reality make a distinction or division between national and local elections more likely. However, no change was achieved in this respect.

2. Legal Status of Different Legal Acts

20. It follows from what has been said above that the Parliament is a unicameral body which is elected in ordinary elections in September every fourth year, with a possibility for extraordinary elections that has until now never been used.

21. According to Chapter 4, Article 1 IG, the Riksdag convenes in session every year. Sessions are held in Stockholm, unless otherwise determined by the Riksdag or the Speaker. As follows from Chapter 1, Article 2 of the Riksdag Act, every parliamentary or Riksdag session continues until the start of the next session, though the starting date of such a session will depend on whether an election has taken place or not. Should that be the case, the Parliament as mentioned *above* will convene on the fifteenth day after election day, while otherwise, in years when no ordinary election is held, a new session starts on a day in September determined by the Parliament in advance (i.e., before its summer recess).[8]

22. The political power rests with the Parliament and in particular the government. Within the government, the prime minister has a very strong position. In fact, the parliament only votes on his nomination and he is then free to choose any members that he wishes for the government.

---

7. Concerning the rules for extraordinary elections in general, it may be noted that they may only be called when three months have passed since the newly-elected Parliament was convened after the former election. The Government is also barred from calling an extraordinary election when its ministers remain at their posts, after they have been formally discharged, pending assumption of office by a new government. *See* Ch. 3, Art. 4, s. 2 for further details.
8. This means that formally speaking, the Parliamentary session (*riksmöte*) is always convened, though it would of course be impossible to ask of the MPs that they should be in session in Stockholm for fifty-two weeks of the year. Instead, the Riksdag Act prescribes (Ch. 2, Art. 6) that the Speaker will determine what breaks of a week or more that shall be made in the work of the Chamber during the current session; normally, the session is for instance interrupted for summer and Christmas breaks and during certain other weeks. He may also decide, upon a request by 115 MPs or by the Government, to interrupt a parliamentary recess, in which case a meeting of the Chamber shall be held within ten days from the submission of such a request.

23. Sweden has a long history as a highly centralized state, a monarchy with Stockholm as its capital and, since circa 1920, a well-functioning parliamentary democracy. It holds no depending or special territories.

24. As is generally known, Sweden joined the European Union (EU) together with Austria and Finland on 1 January 1995. The membership found its legal (and political) support in an accession treaty concluded in February 1994 and a referendum on 13 November 1994, in which 52.4% voted yes while 46.7% voted no. (82% of the registered voters participated in this referendum and it may be noted that only Swedish citizens were allowed to vote, as a contrast to ordinary local elections, but in line with parliamentary elections.)

25. A special feature of the Swedish political system, which is important to keep in mind when analysing or trying to understand it, is the historical dominance at the national level of the Social Democratic Party, that has held on to the governmental power from 1932–1976 (albeit in a coalition with the farmers from 1951–1957), 1982–1991, 1994–2006 and then in a coalition with the Green Party (2014–2022). This situation has few equivalents in other democratic states and would normally increase the risk for corruption, which has however, so far, never been a big problem in Sweden. This fact may have something to do with the Nordic and Swedish tradition of openness in the public administration, as further explained in the text.[9]

26. The same parties that sit in the Parliament also dominate at local and regional level, where some variations are however possible. Also at those levels, the same electoral rules apply, though in a slightly modified form; exact details on this are to be found in the lengthy Electoral Law (Vallagen, 1997:157), in particular its Chapter 18.

27. The existing rules today concerning financial support to political parties are the law on financing or support or aid of political parties (*lagen om insyn i finansiering av partier*, 2018:90). According to that law, parties who receive anonymous contributions over a certain sum (currently SEK 250.000) are not entitled to state support. Apart from that, there has also since 1996 a law on the registration of the economic interests and commitments of the Members of Parliament since 1996 (1996:810), which is however not compulsory but entirely based on voluntary participation of the MPs. According to the law, though, the MPs following the instructions have to reveal their incomes and activities. The idea behind the voluntary participation appears to be that the voters would have less confidence in MPs not participating, but so far, no study has been made on whether this is actually the case.

9. This has recently been identified by the EU Commission in its special anti-corruption report, COM (2014) 38. The organization Reportrar utan gränser (Reporters without borders) in its index of the press freedom in the world of 2024 put Sweden on place 3 in the world concerning the freedom of the press. Factors as the general access to documents were considered strong, while increased surveillance by state security bodies, not least on the internet, were viewed as potential threats against the press freedom. *See* World Press Freedom Index – Reporters Without Borders, available at www.reportrarutangranser.se/rapporter/2014/pressfrihetsindex-2014.

28. However, a governmental committee in 2004 proposed a new law in order to make this whole area more regulated and transparent. The document or report containing this proposal,[10] a new law on the publication of the incomes of political parties and electoral candidates, which was proposed to enter into force on 1 January 2006, may in many ways be seen as a point of departure for the subsequent, lively discussion on those questions. It may be noted that the existing law as well as the various proposed ones that have been discussed are national laws, though their rules do now cover candidates to the national parliament, as well as local and regional assemblies and also the EU Parliament.

29. The proposal from 2006 meant that each party should make an annual public account of its incomes and that, at the same time, each candidate who had been elected to any of the assemblies mentioned above (i.e., a national parliament, a local or regional assembly or the EU Parliament), should be obliged to make a public declaration on how the campaign was financed. This last proposal should be viewed in the light of the increased scope for personal campaigning that has existed since 1998, due to changes in the electoral law.

30. The proposal from 2006 was that the value of each contribution and the name of the donor should be made public if the total contribution during the respective relevant period adds up to a total of SEK 20,000 or more. Here, in 2014, the Constitutional Committee of the Parliament suggested solving this problem by obliging all the parties that are represented there to guarantee that they will not accept anonymous, private support or donations, as a condition for obtaining support from the state.[11] As explained above, this proposal has now been passed.

31. Besides, an agreement between all the main political parties from 1980, confirmed in 2000, means that the parties are obliged to reveal their sources of income at the national level, whenever asked to do so by the media or representatives of the public. Information concerning the economic interests of any member of the government has been public since 1995.

32. No rules exist concerning which persons, organizations, classes or groups of persons or of organizations, if any, are expressly forbidden from contributing. The general rules against bribery and corruption in the penal code will apply should any such crimes be suspected. Those rules have been changed and sharpened in recent years, due to new rules and conventions within the EU and the Council of Europe.

---

10. SOU (Statens Offentliga Utredningar, i.e., Official Government Reports) 2004:22, Allmänhetens insyn i partiers och valkandidaters intäkter (The public openness of the incomes of parties and electoral candidates).
11. KU 2013/14:17. – State support to the parties represented in the Parliament has been paid since the 1960s, in order to stimulate political interest and reduce the risk of corruption. However, also this system has been criticized.

33. No restrictions concerning political campaign activities of civil servants and other public employees exist as such, which is worth noting. This is typically considered a part of the freedom of speech, though it goes without saying that the public confidence in leading civil servants or judges would not survive a strong political bias from any of them.

II. Geography and Population

34. The capital of Sweden is Stockholm. On 1 July, 2024, the population of Sweden amounted to 10,553.300 (10.553.300) persons. The size of the country is 173,732 sq mi (449,963 sq km). Besides France and Spain, Sweden is thus the largest Member State of the EU. The official language is Swedish. Four languages have official status as a minority language, namely Finnish, Hebrew, Sami, and a dialect of Finnish spoken in the border region in the far north between Sweden and Finland. Concerning religion, the protestant belief dominates (87%), while others (roman catholic, orthodox, Baptist, Muslim, Jewish, Buddhist) are shared by 13% of the population. The national or ethnic composition is 80% Swedish, with 20% immigrants of different origins. Sweden is a fairly old country. Its date of independence or creation was 6 June 1523.

III. Social and Cultural Values

35. While the ancient Swedish constitution of 1809 contained only one single article related to human rights, its §16, the FPA of that same year (and then renewed in 1812), offered a wide protection of the freedom of speech exercised in books and journals. Historically, the only way to explain this somewhat privileged and internationally very unusual position of the printed word within the constitutional system and regulation of the country is, undoubtedly, an awareness of the importance that books and journals have always had in the formation of opinions (alongside of the importance of access to documents and transparency within the public administration in order to combat corruption and misuse of power). Since TV and other media have a similar position in today's world, the enactment of FSA in 1992 was also logical from this point of view.

36. This historically strong protection of freedom of speech and information is probably quite unique in an international perspective. It must be said to reflect the interests embedded in these freedoms as deep social and cultural values of the Swedish society, which is of course also characterized by values such as openness, equality and social welfare.

§2. The Media Landscape

I. Overview of Media Markets and Main Actors

37. The public authority for radio and TV matters, Mediemyndigheten, conducts an annual survey of the media use and media production and distribution in Sweden, which contains some very interesting information. The facts presented below are taken from the report of 2024.[12]

38. Here, it is revealed for instance that the average Swede spends no less than seven hours every day consuming media, a figure that must be seen as high. This has gone up from six hours after the covid crisis that started in 2020. However, 'only' 47% do now read a printed daily newspaper, while 40% read this in its digital format.

39. As will be described below in the last section, the concentration of media in the hands of a few owners is actually very high in Sweden and it seems to be a fact that the rather peculiar constitutional regulation of the media sector does in fact contribute to this. The main actors, that are influential in all or at least many areas (TV, radio, internet, press) are Bonniers, an old family empire based in Stockholm. However, in sheer terms, also the Swedish state and the Norwegian media group Schibsted are very big, though the state is active only in TV and radio and Schibsted mainly in the daily press.[13]

II. Broadcasting Infrastructure

A. TV

40. In the TV sector, the four leading companies, Sveriges Television (SVT, public service), TV 4 (Bonniers), MTG and SBS own the TV stations that dominate the market, with a total of 90% of all viewing.[14] Individually, of these, SVT has 36.6% and TV 4 28.9%. Here, a clear concentration of ownership in a few hands is thus visible. While the public service channels show more programmes devoted to information and facts than ever, the tendency in the commercial channels is the opposite.

41. Today, more than 90% of all households have access to various cable-TV services. The basic channels, for which no cable is required, are SVT1, SVT 2, TV 4, TV 6 (MTG) and the so-called SVT *Kunskapskanalen*, a public service channel showing only programmes containing knowledge, facts and education. At the same

12. Mediekonsumtion – Medieutveckling 2024, Mediemyndigheten, Stockholm 2024 (available at www.mediemyndigheten.se).
13. It also manages some important and profitable sites on the internet, such as 'www.blocket.se', where very many Swedes sell and buy various things.
14. Thus, the dominating channels, are the so-called big five: SVT1 (24.3%), SVT2 (6.7%), TV 3 (MTG, 6.4%), TV 4 (18.9%) and finally Kanal 5 (SBS, 6.1%).

time, 81% of the households had signed contracts for digital cable TV-services. The technical conditions for receiving satellite programmes exist, however, in all of Sweden, which means that this figure has recently grown. As shown in the above-mentioned (footnote 12) annual report from Mediemyndigheten, different streaming services are becoming increasingly popular and now reach 76% of the population, while traditional TV channels are gradually losing ground.

42. In 2024, 95% of the households did have access to traditional TV, covering the 'basic channels' mentioned above, which is since 2007 digital but still transmitted 'on the ground'. This is the only kind of transmission that still requires a licence, as explained below. The government decides on this licence, or permission for the public service channels and the Public Authority for radio and TV does the same for the commercial channels. Other models of TV distribution are entirely based on contracts between the TV channels and the distributors or operators.

43. TV is also one of the leading media for advertising, though that position is now being challenged by the internet. In 2012, an estimated 18.6% of all advertising in Sweden took place on TV channels. This is a high figure, given that the public service channels do not contain advertising. (Instead, they are financed by special licence fees[15] and contributions from the state.)

B. Radio

44. Despite a rapid technical development in recent years, in Sweden as in many other countries, it may be observed that radio emissions in Sweden are not yet fully digitalized (as opposed to TV emissions). However, applications for the starting of new, digitalized radio channels have now come to the Government, in particular since it declared, in June 2013, its intention to digitalize the whole radio network.[16] Until that has happened – in 2026, according to the suggestion – only the public service companies are allowed to transmit national radio programmes. Other digital licences are sold at special auctions.

45. The number of radio listeners has decreased ever since 2000, which may partly be due to the growth of Spotify and similar web-based music services. In 2024, 61% of Swedes owned a traditional radio, but while people older than 60 years listened for two hours every day, young people (under 25) did the same, only for 30 minutes. Apart from the public service company, *Sveriges Radio (SR)*, financed by public contributions in the same way as Sveriges Television, all other radio stations are financed by advertisements. Of these totally 103 private operators, in 2013, the 103 licences that were then granted are all geographically limited and cover different parts – but together all – of Sweden. When full digitalization

15. Every owner of a TV or a PC computer is obliged to pay such fees, but needless to say, the supervision is far from perfect.
16. *See* prop 2012/13:164, Bildning och tillgänglighet – radio och TV i allmänhetens tjänst 2014-19. – At the end of 2024, seventy-seven applications had been made for future digital transmissions.

finally happens, the idea is to organize the radio sector slightly differently, with two networks each covering sixteen available radio channels. Both national and regional transmissions will then be possible, in a total of thirty-four regions.

C. *Internet*

46. Concerning the internet, we may here just very briefly observe its growing importance also as a media phenomenon, e.g., by 'new' tendencies such as radio and TV programmes being available there ('web TV', and e.g., streaming services).[17] Understandably, this new situation also has important economic consequences. Thus, advertising on the internet on Swedish sites already in 2012 grew by 9.9%, to a total figure of SEK 7.7 billion (7,700,000,000).

III. Technological and Economic Developments in the Media Markets

47. In 2024, 95% of the households had access to traditional, ground-based TV, 35.4% (though in reality many more, as explained below) had cable, 15.6% satellite and 11.5% internet-based, so-called Ip-TV (which may also come to grow in the future, since the technical conditions are good, with extensive broadband coverage).Only 0.1% lacked television, while 10% could not be totally identified (while obviously watching TV), due to some technical problems. Many households do of course have many of those forms; the statistics are thus not really very revealing here. Still, it is estimated that more than 80% of the houses in which more than one household lives have access, through special networks, to cable channels. It could also be observed that as many as 25% of all persons in the age of 9–79 years have access to TV on their mobile phones.

48. As mentioned above, traditional TV and the basic TV channels were digitalized in 2007, while national radio is still not digitalized but may be so in the near future (presumably in 2026 or 2027). It is thus still too early to analyse exactly how digitalization may affect the media market as a whole.

17. In May 2013, no less than 113 web radio stations were registered by the Public Radio and TV Authority. It is also worth noting that almost all TV companies today have their own TV services displayed on the internet (through so-called play programmes).

Part I. Freedom of Speech

§1. Introduction

49. In order to understand Swedish media law and the very special situation concerning the regulation of freedom of speech in Sweden, a historical perspective is definitely necessary. This may explain why freedom of speech has enjoyed constitutional protection since 1766 and is now being protected by no less than three constitutional Acts – of which two are in fact entirely devoted to freedom of speech. The importance of this particular and somewhat unique tradition becomes even clearer when considering that the Swedish regulation, with the FPA of 1949 regulating books and newspapers and the FSA of 1991[18] dealing with other media, does not only have constitutional status but also regulates almost every important aspect of criminal and procedural law in this area, as well as the main issues related to access to documents and transparency in the public administration (Chapter 2 of FPA). They are thus both very important acts and entirely crucial within this field of law. This also reflects that freedom of speech, as well as freedom of information (in particular the general access to public documents), are profound values of the Swedish society and have been so ever since the end of the eighteenth century.

50. Below, after a historical survey, the content of the three constitutional acts regulating freedom of speech in Sweden will be presented and analysed. Given the highly technical content of FPA and not least FSA and their similar structure, an attempt is made to show the practical importance of many technically complicated rules. After that, in the second section, more attention is given to regulations in the 'outer' sphere of media law, dealing with such things as ownership, establishment of media, advertising, purchases and competition in a way that is hugely influenced and affected by EU law, but may on the other hand also be very different from and therefore come into conflict with parts of EU law. However, since those rules are after all less unique for Sweden and less historically important, they will not be analysed quite as much in detail.

18. In the official translation from the Swedish Parliament (The Constitution of Sweden – The Fundamental Laws and the Riksdag Act, Sveriges Riksdag, Stockholm 2012), this act bears the long name The Fundamental Law on Freedom of Expression, which will however not be used here.

Chapter 1. Historical Background and Current Legal Situation: Freedom of Speech as a Societal Value

51. The first FPA (Tryckfrihetsförordningen) was thus introduced in 1766.[19] After an interruption from 1772, a new FPA with constitutional status was enacted in 1809 and then further modified and modernized in 1812. When that act was perceived as having been misused or even abused by the public authorities under the Second World War, a new one (the current, still existing one) was adopted in 1949.

52. While the ancient Swedish constitution of 1809 contained only one single article related to human rights, its §16, the FPA of that same year (and then renewed in 1812) offered a wide protection of the freedom of speech exercised in books and journals. Until 1 January 1992, when the FSA entered into force, the current FPA enacted in 1949 was analogously applied also on other media than books and journals, the forms of expression for which it is and has always been intended.[20] Historically, the only way to explain this somewhat privileged and internationally very unusual position of the printed word within the constitutional system and regulation of the country is, undoubtedly, an awareness of the importance that books and journals have always had in the formation of opinions (alongside of the importance of access to documents and transparency within the public administration in order to combat corruption and misuse of power). Since TV and other media have a similar position in today's world, the enactment of FSA in 1992 was also logical from this point of view. Subsequently, a number of legislative attempts have been made to merge FPA and FSA into one single act, but all the legislative committees dealing with this issue have arrived at the conclusion that this is simply too difficult and complicated from a technical point of view.[21] Thus, the specific Swedish constitutional tradition in this area looks likely to remain.

53. So, let us now look closer at this tradition. With the first FPA, of 1766, the censorship that had existed since the late seventeenth century was abolished, except as far as religious books and books imported from abroad were concerned. Still, also with these exceptions, this was a radical, progressive and possibly globally unique piece of legislation in the late eighteenth century. It guaranteed the right to anonymity for writers, as well as the principle of access to documents, and stated the right to print any kind of material *except what was clearly prohibited by the express words of FPA*. This latter aspect may have had something to do with the fact that FPA was then gradually limited, due to political upheavals starting with a *coup d'état* leading to a 'restoration' or strengthening of the monarchy in 1772. At least, it may have contributed to this process.

---

19. To print something is in Swedish thus called 'trycka'.
20. In principle, this must have been the case also before 1949, but since other media were then not very important, this was hardly ever discussed.
21. *See* most recently SOU 2010:168, Ny yttrandefrihetsgrundlag? Yttrandefrihetskommittén presenterar tre modeller, a proposal subsequently modified by SOU 2012:55, En översyn av tryck- och yttrandefriheten.

54. A new, 'full' FPA with constitutional status, containing all or almost all the rights mentioned in the first text, did then not occur until 1812, as a result of the changes that also produced the constitution of 1809 – which was, hence, to remain in force until 1974, while the FPA of 1812 was not replaced until 1949, as mentioned above. Both those constitutional acts were thus documents of longevity, while the fact that freedom of speech in books and newspapers were so well protected but other basic human rights hardly mentioned at all in the constitution must be said to reflect a particular Swedish constitutional tradition, still of importance, that stresses freedom of speech (and information) due to its importance for democracy and the free debate, while not paying quite as much attention to other fundamental rights or the need to offer them judicial protection.[22]

55. The FPA of 1812 also prohibited censorship in religious matters and was thus more liberal than its predecessor, but a big problem – which was growing but also lasting, until the Second World War, when its (too) frequent use was the main reason why a new, modernized FPA was considered necessary – was the right for the government, through specific agencies such as the national Post, to simply stop and prohibit the distribution of any controversial or unpopular newspaper. The publishers who were treated this way normally responded by publishing a new, very similar paper or magazine, maybe with a slight change of name, that for the interested reader in fact seemed to be identical with the banned one.[23] For instance, during the Second World War, newspapers were stopped from circulating more than 300 times since the government, acting through the Minister of Justice, thought that their publication – in neutral Sweden – might jeopardize relations with other states(!). Any such attempts are now prohibited by Chapter 6, Article 4 FPA.

56. It was also under the FPA of 1812 – which was, needless to say, changed a number of times between 1812 and 1949 – that many other, very important principles and institutions were established, such as the jury system (in 1815) and the idea that the legal responsibility for the content of a printed work could always be placed on one single individual, as explained below. In fact, this was necessary in order to give the idea of *anonymity* any legal sense. Also, the principle of access to documents was strengthened, under the surveillance of the first so-called *Ombudsman* (*Justitieombudsmannen*, JO), who was also introduced in 1809 (and then became a rather successful Swedish 'constitutional export product'). Gradually, this development also led to the protection of secret informants to the press or, with a

22. When the FPA of 1812 was enacted, this fact, together with the absence of separation of powers in the traditional sense (i.e., as defined by Montesquieu and other contemporary philosophers) in the constitution of 1809 even led to the expression that the media, the press, represented 'the third estate' (*tredje statsmakten*). This highly incorrect manner of speech may sometimes still, unfortunately, be heard in Sweden.

23. The most well-known example was probably the liberal-radical newspaper Aftonbladet in Stockholm, which still exists. Having been prohibited and withdrawn from circulation, it was then republished as Aftonbladet nos 2, 3 et cetera, up until no. 26. As it happens, since this way of stopping newspapers from being circulated was neither efficient nor popular, it was abolished in 1844, but during the Second World War it was replaced with a possibility for the government to prohibit controversial newspapers from being transported on trains, boats and airplanes. After the war, then, this practice was heavily criticized in the public debate, both by media, scholars and politicians.

modern term, *whistleblowers*. It is likely that the still rather low extent of corruption in Sweden owes a lot to this constitutional heritage.[24]

57. During this long time, a number of delimitations were also introduced, clarifying that the FPA could not apply to every single word that was to be found in a written newspaper. Thus, matters related to intellectual property law – that did, at least then, perhaps mainly affect books – were regulated by ordinary law in 1876 and have been so ever since.[25] In 1947, eventually, in the travaux préparatoires for the new FPA, it was also clearly stated and established as a legal fact that the use of the printed word in order to commit crimes such as fraud or forgery should never enjoy the protection of the FPA.[26] Today, a number of delimitations follow directly from FPA (Chapter 1, Articles 11–13),[27] while others have evolved through jurisprudence.[28] Also, other changes occurred gradually; e.g., in 1937, rules both on the jury system and access to documents were thus placed in ordinary laws, alongside the constitutional regulation, in order to make their practical application easier.

58. Needless to say, however, the FPA of 1949 was a considerably more modern document.[29] For instance, as a reaction against a certain oppression of the press during the Second World War,[30] any censorship of the printed word is now totally and unconditionally forbidden, in all matters and at all times (FPA Chapter 1, Article 1 section 2).[31] It has also been clarified that FPA does not apply in a number of situations, e.g., concerning commercial advertisements and, since 1998, in relation to any kind of pornography depicting children (Chapter 1, Article 14).

24. This was recently also pointed out by the EU Commission in its special anti-corruption report, COM (2014) 38.
25. Thus, this is one of few situations where freedom of speech may sometimes be sacrificed in favour of other legal values. A good, though very strange example is the case NJA 1998 s. 848, which concerned the publication of a new Swedish edition and translation of the (in)famous book *Mein Kampf* by Adolf Hitler. Due to specific German legal procedures, the intellectual property right of the book belongs to the Land (State) of Bavaria, that intervened and sought to prevent the publication, with assistance from the Swedish police. After lengthy legal proceedings, publication was eventually stopped and the publisher was sentenced to a fine for violating the Intellectual Property Law (*Upphovsrättslagen*, 1960:729) – despite the fact that Bavaria's 'ownership' of the book was not as such recognized in Sweden. The case is complicated, even in a way absurd, and highly atypical, but nevertheless shows that this is an area where the value as such of freedom of speech is weaker than otherwise.
26. *See* SOU 1947:60 p. 115.
27. Covering except for intellectual property law and child pornography notably various kind of advertisements.
28. Notably in relation to criminal behaviour and commercial advertisements.
29. One author has thus described it as being characterized by a 'sound' or 'wise pessimism', given the harsh experiences of the war, which seems adequate. *See* Anders R. Olsson, Yttrandefrihet & Tryckfrihet – Handbok för journalister, 7th ed, Lund 2013, p. 17.
30. For a more detailed survey on this topic, *see* Nils Funcke, Tryckfriheten – Ordets män och statsmakterna, Stockholm 2006.
31. To make a comparison, we may say that it is now constitutionally abolished in the same way as the death penalty (Ch. 2, Art. 4 IG).

59. Once again, it may be underlined that historically, this somewhat privileged and internationally very unusual position of the printed word within the constitutional regulation of the country is best explained by the awareness of the importance that books and journals have always had in the formation of opinions (and the importance of access to documents and general transparency within the public administration in order to combat corruption and misuse of power). Since TV and other media today have a similar position and importance as books and journals, the enactment of FSA in 1992 was also logical from this point of view.

Chapter 2. The Importance and Role of the Instrument of Government in Relation to Freedom of Speech

60. The first individual right to be mentioned in Chapter 2 of the new constitution of 1974 (*Regeringsformen*, Instrument of Government (IG)) is the freedom of speech or expression (Article 1, section 1, p. 1), which is there defined as the freedom to communicate information and express thoughts, opinions and sentiments, whether orally, pictorially, in writing or in any other way. Since such freedom is protected by FPA and FSA when exercised in different media, it goes without saying that only a limited field of freedom of speech is actually left to be protected 'only' by the IG; what remains, then, are basically opinions, utterances or statements passed between individuals or in small groups, as well as the ones presented at theatre or art performances or at public meetings which are not showed in radio or TV (the latter of which are however also protected by the freedom of assembly in Chapter 2, Article 1, section 1, pp. 3–4).[32] Also, regular internet communication is covered mainly by IG.

61. Still, such utterances with a limited reach may have great legal significance, as shown most recently by the so-called *Manga* case of 2012, which concerned possession of some forty drawn Japanese art pictures of naked, pre-pubertal youngsters. In this case, the owner was a professional translator who also worked with censorship, but since 1998, any possession of such material is illegal and FPA will never apply in relation to such material (Chapter 1, Article 14). Nevertheless, the Supreme Court here used the rules on freedom of speech and freedom of information in IG, including the rules determining when these freedoms may be limited (Chapter 2 Articles 21 and 23) to decide that his possession of the material was justified, while stressing the difference between drawn art of this kind, depicting kids that were not recognizable and – with one exception – not even realistically portrayed, and on the other hand photos or paintings based on living models. While the owner was thus sentenced to a fine by two lower courts, he was in the end acquitted by the Supreme Court.[33]

62. In this respect, it may also be mentioned that freedom of information stands in such a close connection to freedom of speech that it may even be described as its flipside.[34] In Chapter 2, Article 1, section 1, p. 2 IG, freedom of information is described as the freedom to procure and receive information and otherwise acquaint oneself with the utterances of others, but it is worth underlining that it does not include the access to documents covered by Chapter 2 of the FPA, as emphasized

32. *See also* Nergelius, Svensk statsrätt, p. 118. For all those freedoms of opinions now mentioned, certain restrictions apply concerning how and when they may be restricted by law. Most importantly, this may only take place for certain purposes and a small parliamentary minority may urge that any such proposed limitation shall abide one year before entering into force; *see* IG Ch. 2, Arts 20–24. It may be noted that these requirements may also be applied when limitations of the freedom of speech covered by FSA do occur; *see* Ch. 3, Art. 5 FSA.
33. *See* NJA (Nytt Juridiskt Arkiv) 2012 p. 400.
34. It is e.g., so described by prop (i.e., *law bill*) 1975/76:209, at p. 110.

by the last section of Chapter 2, Article 1 IG. Access to documents thus forms another kind of freedom of information all on its own, more specific to Sweden, so to speak.

63. According to Chapter 1, Articles 5–6 of the FPA, the Act applies to all written matters produced with a printing press that are *edited,*[35] provided that certain formal and technical conditions are fulfilled.[36] It does however not apply to every word that is to be found in such material, as will be further explained below.

64. There are now, thus, three different kinds of freedom of speech in Swedish constitutional law, namely the ones covered respectively by the IG, the FPA and the FSA, while at the same time a certain kind of statements or utterances do by definition fall outside all those three acts, namely the ones that are simply criminal, for instance because they are a part of a fraud or some other crime. Certain other limitations of the strengthened protection of freedom of speech that FPA does indeed provide are also envisaged by its Chapter 1, Article 9, particularly in relation to commercial advertising.[37]

35. In Swedish, this key word is called 'utgiven'. The requirements for this criterion to be met are quite difficult and will not be dealt with here. However, basically it means that a book or newspaper must have been handed over to a distributor, but whether the distribution has in fact started doesn't really matter. – Concerning the definition of what is a printed work, *see* FPA Ch 1, Art. 7.

36. In this respect, *see also* Ch. 1, Art. 7.

37. While such advertising that does also contain some message of an ideological or other kind does normally, according to settled jurisprudence, fall within the scope of FPA. Further limitations are made in relation to rules on copyright and intellectual property, Ch. 1, Art. 8, as well as for child pornography, Ch. 1, Art. 14, as mentioned above.

Chapter 3. Freedom of Speech as Defined by the Freedom of Press Act

65. Certain important definitions of what freedom of press means are found already in Chapter 1, Article 1 FPA. Thus, the freedom of the press is defined in Chapter 1, Article 1, section 1 as the right of every Swedish citizen to publish any written matter, without prior hindrance by any public authority, and not to be prosecuted thereafter on grounds of its content, other than before a lawful court (using a special jury system, as explained below), or punished therefore for any other reason than because the content contravenes an express provision of law. This may be described as the essence of the *exclusive* character of FPA, meaning that it regulates any possible use of the printed word.[38]

66. Perhaps even more important is section 2 of that same article, according to which, in order to secure the free exchange of opinion and availability of comprehensive information, every Swedish citizen shall be free, subject to the rules in FPA, to express his thoughts and opinions in print, to publish official documents and communicate information and intelligence to journalists on any subject whatsoever (so-called *meddelarfrihet*, which is wide and internationally very unusual).[39]

67. In line with this, no scrutiny of any written matter prior to printing may exist according to Chapter 1, Article 8, which also states that no actions not authorized under the FPA are allowed for the authorities in order to prevent the printing, publication or dissemination of any written matter due to its content.[40]

68. Chapter 1, Article 10 contains the so-called *Instruction*, which judges and jurors are supposed to observe when passing judgment on abuses of the freedom of the press. This article states that they should then constantly bear in mind the connection between the freedom of the press and its role in a free society, directing attention 'always more to illegality of subject matter and thought than to illegality of expression, to the aim rather than the manner of presentation' and, in case of doubt, acquit rather than convict.

---

38. With the exceptions mentioned above in relation to criminal activities, child pornography, advertisements (*see* here also Ch. 7, Art. 2) and some other matters (e.g., disputes on intellectual property).
39. According to Ch. 7, Art. 21, it does however not apply in relation to some special crimes such as fraud espionage and deliberate disregard of a duty of confidentiality. For others than Swedish citizens, certain limitations through law are possible according to Ch. 14, Art. 5.
40. *See also* Ch. 1, Arts 1 and 9, which state that no person may be prosecuted or held liable under penal law or subject to any other sanctions on account of an abuse of the freedom of the press other than as prescribed by the FPA.

Chapter 4. European Human Rights Law on Freedom of Speech

69. Treaties entered into by Sweden do not form part of Swedish constitutional law and are in fact not a part of Swedish law at all until they have been incorporated or transformed into Swedish national law. In other words, Sweden, together with other Nordic countries, traditionally has a dualistic view on the relationship between national and international law.

70. This situation may be illustrated by the fate of the European Convention of Human Rights (ECHR) in Swedish law. Sweden ratified this convention already in 1951 (although the jurisdiction of European Court of Human Rights (ECtHR) was not acknowledged until 1966), but it was not incorporated into Swedish national law until 1995, when Sweden joined the EU. Thus, for forty-five years, the Convention was never a part of Swedish law and could strictly speaking not be invoked in proceedings before Swedish national courts. However, it was nevertheless used by high Swedish courts and by the Supreme Court in particular as a means of interpretation, especially in the late 1980s and the early 1990s, when Sweden had been condemned for violations in a number of cases before the Strasbourg court. This meant that this particular convention came to have a certain, or rather considerable, importance in Swedish law before even being incorporated, but that is a clear exception from the main, general rule.

71. Sweden is, thus, like the other Nordic states, a typical example of what is normally called a dualist state in terms of its relations with international law, i.e., a state where international law, whether in the terms of international customary law or of international conventions that Sweden has duly ratified, does not take effect within the national legal system without a special act of transformation that turns them into domestic law.[41] During the 1980s, however, the two highest Swedish courts gradually came to consider ECHR as an important source of interpretation and inspiration.[42] Swedish laws were thus interpreted in the light of ECHR and the case-law from ECtHR.[43]

72. The next step in the development, then, came in 1994, when it was decided that when joining the EU, Sweden should also incorporate ECHR into national law. Also here, Sweden walked almost hand in hand with the other Nordic countries.

73. The incorporation took effect as of 1 January 1995, which was of course not coincidental.[44] By incorporating ECHR at the same time that Sweden was going to

---

41. From a legal point of view, this fact, in relation to ECHR, was acknowledged in two cases in the early 1970s from the Supreme Court and the Supreme Administrative Court respectively; *see* NJA 1973, p. 423 and RÅ 1974, p. 121.
42. For a general comment, *see* Iain Cameron, An Introduction to the European Convention on Human Rights, 6th ed. Uppsala 2011.
43. *See* e.g., cases NJA 1988 p. 572, 1989 p. 131, 1990 p. 636, 1991 p. 188 and p. 512, as well as RÅ (the Supreme Administrative Court) 1990 ref. 75.
44. The travaux préparatoires are to be found in the Governmental Bill (SOU) 1993:40, Parts A and B, but also in prop 1993/94:117 p. 37 s., as well as KU 1993/94:24 p. 19 s.

join the EU, situations where the question of whether the Convention would be applied or not, should depend on whether EU law was applicable were avoided.[45]

74. However, the incorporation nevertheless took place in a problematic way, in particular from a legal point of view. Due to a political compromise, the ECHR, despite being referred to in IG Chapter 2, Article 19 (former Article 23, until 2011), was never given a constitutional status, but is as such incorporated through ordinary law.[46] IG Chapter 2, Article 19 simply states that 'no act of law or other provision may be adopted' that contravenes Sweden's obligations under ECHR. This may of course be seen as a rule directed to the legislator rather than to the courts.[47] The situation, should a law passed either before or after 1 January 1995 be in conflict with the ECHR, was in the *travaux préparatoires* handed to the courts to deal with through ordinary means of legislative interpretation, such as rules on, e.g., *lex posterior* and *lex specialis*.[48] However, an important change in IG Chapter 11, Article 14, taking effect as of 1 January 2011, gives the courts greater scope for judicial review of unconstitutional laws in general, which might also make them bolder in relation to ECHR.[49]

75. Still, which is perhaps not entirely surprising against this background, the Swedish courts have so far often been rather reluctant to use the ECHR, at least when this would mean setting aside a national law. In one case from 1998,[50] the Supreme Court even refused to uphold the Convention (as well as the FSA) against a demand from Swedish and Norwegian authorities to execute a penal judgment from a Norwegian court (which was all the more embarrassing since Norway was six months later condemned by EctHR for violating the ECHR concerning that same issue).[51]

---

45. The difference that the applicability of EU law may in fact have in a given case was however shown in the crucial *Lassagård* case from 1997 (RÅ 1997 ref. 65), which was decided 1997 in a totally different way by the Supreme Administrative Court, now setting a Swedish law aside, than in a previous case (*Stallknecht*, NJA 1994 p. 657 (Supreme Court) and RÅ 1995 ref. 58), that concerned almost identical issues arising before Sweden's entry into the EU.
46. The number of which is 1994:1500.
47. Cfr Cameron, *supra*, p. 155 ss, as well as Bernitz, European Law in Sweden, p. 81 ss (Ch. 5 of the book, which is called The Incorporation of the European Human Rights Convention into Swedish Law – A half Measure).
48. *See* prop 1993/94:117 p. 37 s., as well as KU 1993/94:24 p. 19 s.
49. For a recent comment, *see* Nergelius, 'Constitutional Reform in Sweden: Some Important Remarks', in *Tijdschrift voor Constitutioneel Recht,* 2013 pp. 372–379.
50. NJA 1998, p. 817.
51. *Bladet Tromsö and Stensaas v. Norway*, 21980/93, Judgment 20 May 1999, ECHR 1999-III, Hudoc ref. 1216. The Swedish Supreme Court held that a Norwegian criminal sentence against a person, Mr Odd Lindberg of Norwegian origin, who had criticized the Norwegian whale hunt in a Swedish TV programme (that was seen by very many Norwegians), could be executed in Sweden since it didnot violate so-called *ordre public*. However, according to the Swedish constitutional act FSA, Lindberg was not legally responsible for his comments, which of course means that the Norwegian judgment against him should not have been recognized, since it was clearly unconstitutional from a Swedish point of view.

76. The same tendency was very clear in the well-known case *Åke Green* of 2005, concerning a reverend who in a sermon denounced homosexuals and their whole life-style, using harsh language; this was contrary to Swedish criminal law, but instead of stating that the national law violated rules on freedom of speech in IG and/or ECHR, the Supreme Court acquitted Green by using long references to various cases from ECtHR, thus indicating that if Green was to be sentenced, Sweden could in a subsequent trial before ECtHR be found guilty of violating the Convention.[52] This cautious attitude may of course be criticized, since the Supreme Court ought to state what the law actually means, rather than speculate on what may happen many years later, in another court.

77. In a more recent case, described in more detail below, the City Court of Uppsala held in December 2013 that both FPA and FSA are superior to ECHR in case of conflict (that might in fact exist in the case).[53] The Court of Appeal of Stockholm reversed the case on 26 November 2014.[54]

78. At the same time, both the highest courts have been very clear in terms of acknowledging, e.g., the impact of the principle of proportionality, flowing from ECHR.[55] Thus, it seems to be easier for the courts to give effect to ECHR through indirect means than to confront Swedish laws directly with the Convention. And for the further presentation, we may keep in mind not only that the jurisprudence of ECtHR and European Court of Justice (ECJ) in matters related to the media and freedom of speech is also binding for and applicable in Sweden but also that Article 10 ECHR is very similar to the protection of freedom of speech offered in Chapter 2 IG.

52. NJA 2005 p. 805.
53. Judgment of 23 Dec. 2013, Case T 1958-12.
54. Case No T 803-14.
55. *See* e.g., NJA 2001 p. 409.

Chapter 5. The Structure and Content of the Freedom of Press Act

§1. GENERAL REMARKS

79. Having the above-mentioned facts in mind, there is obviously no lack within Chapter 1 of FPA of general, principled statements in favour of and aiming at protecting the freedom of expression. But in its remaining Chapters 2–14, the emphasis is on administrative, criminal, procedural and even some civil law rules.

80. Thus, the freedom to print and disseminate printed works is protected through Chapter 4, section 1 and Chapter 6, section 1 FPA,[56] while the freedom of information is protected, except through the rules on access to documents in the lengthy Chapter 2 and the special secrecy act,[57] also through rules on the right to anonymity in Chapter 3. Thus, under Chapter 3, Article 1, an author of any printed matter or a person who has communicated information shall not be obliged to have his name or pseudonym set out therein. Furthermore, according to Chapter 3, Article 2, it shall not be permitted for anyone to inquire into the identity of an author or a person who has communicated information in a case relating to an offence against the freedom of the press, nor to inquire into the identity of the editor of non-periodical printed matter.[58] Similarly, a person who has been active in the production or publication of printed matter, or in an enterprise for the publication of such matter, or an enterprise that professionally purveys news or other material to periodicals, may not disclose what has come to his knowledge in this capacity concerning the identity of an author or a person who has communicated information.[59] This is thus one part of a system with so-called whistleblowers, to use a modern word, that may be said to be constitutionally protected in Sweden (though the system has deeper historical roots than that expression may indicate).

81. Foreigners are basically equal to Swedes as far as the interpretation and application of the rules of FPA are concerned, as follows from Chapter 14, Article 5. The Act itself, however, contains a number of important rules which do reserve certain rights, i.e., to edit printed matter (Chapter 4, Article 1 and Chapter 6, Article 1) to Swedish citizens, which may be doubtful from an EU law perspective. Once

---

56. *See* in this respect also Ch. 5, Arts 4–7.
57. Offentlighets- och sekretesslagen (OSL, 2009:400). According to FPA, Ch. 2, s. 1, every Swedish citizen shall be entitled to free access to official documents, in order to encourage a free exchange of opinions and the availability to comprehensive information. That right may be restricted for certain purposes enumerated in Ch. 2, Art. 2, after which follow, in the rest of the chapter (Arts 3–18) a number of definitions of what is and what is not to be considered a document.
58. Only if, where non-periodical printed matters are concerned, the author or editor has been identified on the publication by name, or by means of a pseudonym or pen-name known generally to refer to a particular person, or if a person has acknowledged in a written statement that he is the author or editor, or has voluntarily made such a declaration before a court of law during the case, may the question of whether he is liable be considered during the procedure.
59. The same rules do apply also for editors of any non-periodical printed matter.

again, according to Chapter 14, Article 5 FPA and Chapter 11, Article 1 FSA, foreigners are equal to Swedish citizens in the application of the two acts, unless otherwise provided by law (i.e., by ordinary laws, which may here make certain exceptions for foreigners, obviously).

82. Here, we may also note that FPA applies mainly, and typically, to books and newspapers that are both printed and edited in Sweden. It will however also apply to newspapers and books that are printed abroad but still edited in Sweden.[60] The freedom of messengers and whistleblowers, however, also applies in relation to foreign books or newspapers.[61] Concerning FSA, the rules are somewhat more complicated here, as explained below.

83. The doubts on the situation for foreigners do however not include the special liability rules in Chapter 8, which follow after the somewhat lengthy enumeration of the crimes that are punishable under the FPA, i.e., when they are committed through a written work, in its Chapter 7.[62] These liability rules are based on the idea that one person may always be held responsible, be it the editor, the author or someone else and that in this so-called chain of responsibility thus established, if one, primarily liable person may not be found, the responsibility will then pass over to someone else, who is next in line. Another point of departure here is that the person held responsible shall have had a good or at least fair chance to know, control and even correct the content before its publication or distribution.

60. *See* FPA Ch. 13, Arts 1–3.
61. *See* FPA Ch. 13, Arts 1–3.
62. This list ranges from high treason and espionage to agitation against a population group, defamation, unlawful threats and deliberate setting aside of a duty of confidentiality.

Chapter 6. The Freedom of Speech Act

84. It may be stressed here again that it could historically seem strange that while the freedom of speech exercised in a certain form, i.e., through written words in printed works, enjoyed constitutional protection already in 1766, no other kind of freedom of speech was even mentioned in any constitutional act until more than two centuries later, i.e., in 1974. The main reason for this is of course not only that other media than the printed word did for a long time simply not exist but also that a rather strong resistance towards any ideas of censorship became evident in the eighteenth century. Legally, this led to a focus on the printed word that would last for more than two centuries. However, the gradual technological development made the situation awkward and a number of governmental committees launched bills and proposals before the FSA was finally enacted in 1991, entering into force on 1 January 1992.

85. The content, structure and functions of FSA[63] are in fact very similar to and entirely based on FPA.[64] Still, some differences between them do of course exist. For instance, according to Chapter 1, Article 1, section 1 FSA, its aim is to guarantee every Swedish citizen, *vis-à-vis* the public institutions, the right publicly to express his thoughts, opinions and sentiments, and in general to communicate information on any subject whatsoever on sound radio, television and certain similar transmissions, films, video recordings, sound recordings and other technical recordings. In other words, the highly technical nature of the act is revealed already here, though the following text talks mainly of radio programmes (a term that, according to Chapter 1, Article 1, section 3, does also, surprisingly enough, include TV programmes), films and sound recordings. Also, the purpose of the freedom of expression protected under the act is defined in a similar way as in FPA, though Chapter 1, Article 1, section 2 of FSA also mentions the freedom of artistic creation.[65]

86. Should any significant difference between the two acts be identified, it is probably that the number of persons protected by FSA could sometimes or even normally be larger, since it is likely to include both the artist or producer of a work that is performed in some of the thus protected media (like, e.g., the director of a film, the composer of a song or the writer of a play) and the performers themselves (the singer, actors or the person being interviewed in a TV programme, as well as the

63. Which in the official translation from the Swedish Parliament bears the long title the Fundamental Law on Freedom of Expression, that will however not be used here.
64. Of the many unfruitful and unsuccessful proposals that have emerged throughout the years to merge them into one single constitutional document, we may here mention SOU 2006:96, Ett nytt grundlagsskydd för tryck- och yttrandefriheten.
65. Which may be justified by the fact that typical films and sound recordings will normally tend to have a limited impact on the formation of opinion.

programme host).[66] This fact, which becomes clear when the rules are analysed in detail, is however not mentioned in the text.[67]

87. It is also noteworthy that FSA seems to cover more – and more varied – forms of expression, such as, apart from radio, TV and films, also webpages (provided that they are managed by professional news agencies or otherwise that they have a so-called editor's proof (*utgivningsbevis)*),[68] publically broadcasted renditions from computers and other technical renditions (e.g., computer games). On the other hand, communication through walkie-talkies or loudspeakers at public stadiums is not covered by the act.[69]

88. In fact, one of the first legal issues to cause a real controversy in Sweden in 2014 concerned such a webpage, called Lexbase, whose idea was to publish all judgments in criminal cases from Swedish courts during the last five years and then make the whole judgments (i.e., not only the names of the parties) available to any interested person who would be willing to pay a small sum for the information. Since these judgments are already public acts, no crime was committed and since the webpage has an 'utgivningsbevis', no public authority could intervene.[70] The head of the Computer Surveillance Agency (*Integritetsskyddsmyndigheten*, formerly known as Datainspektionen) called for a change of FSA Chapter 1, Article 9 in order to make it possible for the authority to act against such websites, that may cause damage to the integrity of individuals, but since this was eight months before the general election in September 2014 and any constitutional change must be announced in the Parliament nine months before the election (*see* IG Chapter 8, Article 14) this could not occur before 2018. It may of course be put into question

66. *See* e.g., NJA 2005 p. 884, where this became very clear.

67. A further difference is that the possibilities to restrict commercial broadcasting are more far-reaching under FSA, as follows notably from its Ch. 1, Art. 12, s. 2. This issue is however technically extremely complicated.

68. *See* FSA Ch. 1, Arts 5–6. This means that for private persons working with their own webpages, the legal situation will be quite different depending on whether they have such a licence, in which case they are covered by the FSA, or not, as explained by Olsson, *supra* p. 35 ss. A practical example of this was given in a judgment by the Supreme Court of 28 Feb. 2014 (case T 1427-12, now published ass NJA 2014 p. 94), where the fact that a webpage lacked such a license made it impossible to order it, or impose upon it, a duty to make available, for thirty days, certain facts related to a previous court case. In this case, thus (but normally not) the lack of a license was in a way beneficial for the webpage in question.

69. This follows, at least indirectly, from Ch. 1, Art. 6 FSA.

70. However, due to public outburst, the webpage or site was temporarily closed on 30 Jan. 2014. – In the, for many reasons, quite controversial judgment of Uppsala City Court in December 2013 (T 1958-12) it was also held that webpages who are not covered by Ch. 1, Art. 9, since they are based abroad and lack an 'utgivningsbevis', could nevertheless enjoy constitutional protection due to an alleged, so-called umbrella effect of FSA. Also this is however controversial and it seems unlikely that higher courts will decide in this way. The Court of Appeal did not elaborate on this point in its judgment of 26 Nov. 2014 (T 803-14).

whether private webpages should so relatively easy be able to enjoy the same constitutional protection as newspapers and TV or radio stations and in 2022 their freedom was curtailed through a change in Chapter 1, Article 20 oFSA, according to which they may be prohibited by law.[71]

89. A few specific differences between FSA and FPA should also be mentioned here. Thus, prior scrutiny and censorship are forbidden according to Chapter 1, Article 11 FSA, though provisions may still under its Article 12 be laid down in law concerning the scrutiny and approval of moving pictures in films, video recordings or other technical recordings intended for public showing. Such prior scrutiny is thus still possible and in fact does exist in Sweden, which may be slightly surprising (though censorship for adults was as such abolished in 2010).[72] On the other hand, the protection against censorship under FSA also includes the right for everyone to *possess* radios and TVs (Chapter 1, Article 13, section 3), which is of course likely to reinforce the freedom of information.

90. Also, the rules on responsibility for the utterances made are slightly different in FSA. In Chapter 4, Article 1, it is stated that an editor must be appointed for any kind of programme or transmission. He or she must, according to Chapter 4, Article 2, be an adult residing in Sweden who is not bankrupt. It must be clear from the copy or technical reproduction of the programme who this person is (Chapter 4, Article 4). Failures to comply with these rules are criminalized (Chapter 4, Article 7). Through Chapter 6, Articles 1–2 FSA, it is also clarified that the editor (or the person who should have appointed an editor but failed to do so) bears the criminal responsibility for any violations of the rules protecting freedom of speech within the FSA.[73] In other words, the so-called chain of responsibility is here shorter than in FPA.

71. Such a prohibition was then approved by the Supreme Administrative Court in 2024 (HFD 2024 ref. 43).
72. Thus, censorship does now, in theory as well as in practice, apply only to kids under 15 years of. – In the more technical sphere, it should also be mentioned that public authorities may according to Ch. 1, Art. 3, s. 3 FSA not prohibit or prevent the possession or employment of such technical aids as are necessary in order to receive radio programmes or comprehend the content of technical recordings on grounds of the content of a radio programme or technical recordings, or ban the construction of landmine networks for the transmission of radio programmes, except by virtue of FSA itself. In at least a principled way, this rule will further strengthen the freedom of information.
73. This is a fact that the Swedish Supreme Court apparently failed to observe in the case NJA 1998 p. 817, where it held that a Norwegian criminal sentence against a person, Mr Odd Lindberg of Norwegian origin, who had criticized the Norwegian whale hunt in a Swedish TV programme (that was seen by very many Norwegians, could be executed in Sweden since it didn't violate so-called *ordre public*). However, according to the Swedish constitutional act FSA, Lindberg was not legally responsible for his comments, which of course means that the Norwegian judgment against him should not have been recognized. It may also be mentioned that shortly afterwards, Norway was held responsible by ECtHR for violating Art. 10 of ECHR in a very similar case; *see Bladet Tromsö and Stensaas v. Norway*, 21980/93, Judgment 20 May 1999, ECHR 1999-III, Hudoc ref. 1216.

Part II. Regulation of Print Media

Chapter 1. The Journalists' Profession

91. A journalist is very rarely held responsible for what is published in a newspaper, which fits well with the fact that the position of the journalist is as such quite informal in Sweden. While special schools of journalism do of course exist, the exercise of this profession does not require any special license or education. Thus, anyone who may want to call himself a journalist is free to do so.[74]

74. The same is true for bloggers, who are also totally unregulated (although criminal rules on e.g., libel do of course also apply to them).

Chapter 2. Journalists' Rights

§1. Role of Journalists as Watchdogs of Society

92. The role of journalists as so-called watchdogs of society is not explicitly formulated anywhere in the Swedish legislation or in any ethical code for the media, but may be traced behind some of the key formulations and definitions in Chapter 1 of FPA. This is the case concerning Chapter 1, Article 1, section 2, which talks about a free exchange of opinions and availability of multi-faceted, pluralistic, comprehensive information as key elements of the freedom of press (or literally freedom to print, *trycka*). As follows from its Chapter 1, Article 1, FSA rests on the same ideas. Of importance here is also the so-called Instruction in FPA Chapter 1, Article 10 (*see also* FSA Chapter 1, Article 15), which states that judges and jurors in cases where any of the two constitutional acts are applied shall always consider that the freedom of speech is fundamental for a free society.

§2. Journalists' Independence

93. The initial articles of both FPA (Chapter 1, Article 1) and FSA (Chapter 1, Articles 1–2) do guarantee freedom of speech for everyone, as well as the right of informants or whistleblowers to pass on information to the media. Any legal interpretation of those articles reveals that they also include a freedom of establishment as such for media companies, with a partial exception for radio and TV transmissions in Chapter 3 FSA (which is discussed in the next section).

94. In other words, this wide freedom of expression must be the point of departure for any legal analysis. In such an analysis, we must also include that neither of the two constitutional acts today covers typical or 'traditional' internet communication. Instead, both acts are based on the traditional assumption that what deserves protection is communication sent from one person or company to a (more or less) wide audience.[75] 'Normal' internet communication may (normally) be protected by IG, but does not otherwise enjoy constitutional protection.

95. Apart from the exceptions described above, where some important delimitations in FSA and FPA make it clear that certain kinds of utterances fall outside their scope or that certain legal issues related to them may be regulated in another way than the one prescribed by these two constitutional acts,[76] it is thus clear that both those two constitutional acts protect and thus apply to any kind of content that is printed in books or journals or presented in any of the different media mentioned

75. *See* Wiweka Warnling-Nerep & Hedvig Bernitz, *En orientering i tryckfrihet & yttrandefrihet*, 5th ed., Stockholm (Jure) 2013 p. 126.

76. According to Ch. 1, Arts 8–10 FPA and Ch. 1, Arts 12–13 FSA, this is now the case concerning commercial advertisements, matters related to information on the financial situation and (in)solvency of individuals, rules on legal responsibility for informants ('whistleblowers') for the way in which they have gathered information and, finally, any display of any kind of child pornography.

in FSA (i.e., what we may describe as *public utterances*). This also means, however, that any kind of legal action brought against any media – or against the author of a book – will have to follow the procedural and penal rules in those two acts, which thus have in a way 'monopolized' this whole field from a legal point of view.[77] The content of the utterances will not affect this fact, but is on the other hand likely to determine whether a specific utterance is legal or not.

§3. Protection of Journalistic Sources

96. Thus, the freedom to print and disseminate printed works is protected through Chapter 4, section 1 and Chapter 6, section 1 FPA,[78] while the freedom of information is protected, except through the rules on access to documents in the lengthy Chapter 2 and the special secrecy act,[79] also through rules on the right to anonymity in Chapter 3. Thus, under Chapter 3, Article 1, an author of any printed matter or a person who has communicated information shall not be obliged to have his name or pseudonym set out therein. Furthermore, according to Chapter 3, Article 2, it shall not be permitted for anyone to inquire into the identity of an author or a person who has communicated information in a case relating to an offence against the freedom of the press, nor to inquire into the identity of the editor of non-periodical printed matter.[80] Similarly, a person who has been active in the production or publication of printed matter, or in an enterprise for the publication of such matter, or an enterprise that professionally purveys news or other material to periodicals, may not disclose what has come to his knowledge in this capacity concerning the identity of an author or a person who has communicated information.[81] This is thus one part of a system with so-called whistleblowers, to use a modern word, that may be said to be constitutionally protected in Sweden (though the system has deeper historical roots than that expression may indicate, as explained below).

97. The right of informants and whistleblowers to pass on information to the media is not only considerably younger than the right of access to documents but also firmly rooted in the constitutional tradition and fulfilling the same tasks, as

77. Normally, in the doctrine, this is expressed by describing those two acts as 'exclusive' within their respective areas of law. A study entirely devoted to this topic is Gunnar Persson, Exklusivitetsfrågan: Om förhållandet mellan tryckfrihet, yttrandefrihet och annan rätt, Stockholm 2002.
78. *See* in this respect also Ch. 5, Arts 4–7.
79. Offentlighets- och sekretesslagen (OSL, 2009:400). According to FPA, Ch. 2, s. 1, every Swedish citizen shall be entitled to free access to official documents, in order to encourage a free exchange of opinions and the availability to comprehensive information. That right may be restricted for certain purposes enumerated in Ch. 2, Art. 2, after which follow, in the rest of the chapter (Arts 3–18) a number of definitions of what is and what is not to be considered a document.
80. Only if, where non-periodical printed matters are concerned, the author or editor has been identified on the publication by name, or by means of a pseudonym or pen-name known generally to refer to a particular person, or if a person has acknowledged in a written statement that he is the author or editor, or has voluntarily made such a declaration before a court of law during the case, may the question of whether he is liable be considered during the procedure.
81. The same rules do apply also for editors of any non-periodical printed matter.

stated above. From a strictly legal point of view, it may be seen in connection with the rule of individual responsibility for any crime described above, thus indicating that not only the informer himself but also other persons who were involved in passing on the information to the writer or the journalist (including, e.g., printers and newspaper stores) are protected from any legal sanctions.[82]

98. The right as such for anyone to pass on information to any media is mentioned in Chapter 1, Article 1, section 2 FPA and Chapter 1, Article 1 FSA.[83] It presupposes, however, that two criteria are met, namely that the information is passed on to someone within a certain category of persons and that this is done with the intention that it shall and will eventually be published.[84] In combination with the individual responsibility, leading to a total absence of sanctions for other persons, this is the essence of the so-called *freedom for messengers* (meddelarfrihet). With the limitations mentioned below, it also applies in relation to foreign media (Chapter 13, Article 1 FPA).

99. However, this wide right also has certain limitations. Certain crimes have been considered to be so important that they will eliminate the general absence of criminal responsibility for the messenger. According to Chapter 7, Article 22 FPA and Chapter 5, Articles 3–4 FSA, this is the case in relation to some very serious crimes such as espionage and deliberate disregard of a duty of confidentiality. In such a situation, but not otherwise, there may also be a possibility for the state, acting through the Chancellor of Justice, to examine who the messenger was (Chapter 3, Article 4 together with Chapter 9, Article 2 section 3 FPA, *see also* Chapter 2, Articles 4–5 FSA). Furthermore, the freedom of messengers does not apply in relation to purely criminal actions (e.g., theft, burglary, deceit) through which the messenger may have gotten hold of the information.[85]

100. These rules were also applied in the above-mentioned case decided by the City Court of Uppsala in December 2013, which caused widespread controversy. This case dealt with a TV recording from a hospital in Uppsala, showing the doctors and nurses at work (a kind of reality show, in other words). In one programme, the struggle of a dying patient was shown in a way that made it possible at least for his family to identify him. His relatives then sued the hospital administration, claiming financial compensation on the (primary) ground that the nurses had deliberately

82. Cfr Hans-Gunnar Axberger, Yttrandefrihetsgrundlagarna, Stockholm 2012 p. 140.
83. Also the right as such to search for and provide information is now protected through Ch. 1, Art. 1, s. 4 FPA, enacted in 1976 as a result of the so-called IB case in the 1970s (*see* below). However, this does not apply should the provision of information have taken place through the use of criminal methods such as theft; *see* Ch. 1, Art. 9 FPA and Ch. 1 Art. 12 FSA.
84. Thus, if the messenger will also pass on the information to some other person, he will be criminally liable for that action according to ordinary law.
85. *See* FPA Ch. 1, Art. 9 p. 5. – In 2012, the newspaper Expressen was held responsible when its reporters had purchased two rifles in Malmö and then handed them over directly to the police, before writing an article revealing how easy it was for anyone to get hold of a weapon in that allegedly crime-ridden city. Here, the way to provide material for the article was considered to be criminal as such, but in 2013, the Supreme Court has decided to try the case in order to find out whether the public interest in knowing about the situation outweighs the – not extremely serious – crime committed.

disregarded their duty of confidentiality. Also the personal dignity in Article 8 of ECHR was invoked, but in a rather surprising move, the City Court found that the nurses, who had been duly informed about the TV recording, had had every reason to believe that the TV company would edit the programme in a way that could not lead to any violation of the rights and dignity of the dying patient. Thus, they had not misused their freedom as messengers, despite the wording of Chapter 5, Article 3 FSA, and in cases of conflict, the Court, as stated above, held that the FSA takes priority over ECHR. The fact that the programme was sent from the United Kingdom did not change the legal situation (cfr Chapter 1, Article 3 FSA). As mentioned, however, the higher instances did not arrive at the same conclusions.

101. Also, the rules on (the right to) anonymity have a relation to the freedom of informers and may hence be analysed from that perspective. Thus, under Chapter 3, Article 1 FPA, an author of printed matter or a person who has communicated information shall not be obliged to have his name or pseudonym set out therein, as mentioned above. Furthermore, according to Chapter 3, Article 2, it shall not be permitted for anyone to inquire into the identity of an author or a person who has communicated information in a case relating to an offence against the freedom of the press, nor to inquire into the identity of the editor of any non-periodical printed matter.[86] The exception in Chapter 3, Article 4 mentioned above is thus a very clear exception, for special cases only, but at the same time, it must be underlined that this general prohibition to search for sources or informers in Chapter 3, FPA and Chapter 2, Article 5 FSA applies only in the public sector, for public bodies.[87] In private companies, executive directors or managers may try to reveal who has leaked sensitive information, although this is a very controversial issue.[88] In the same way, interested private persons may try to investigate the identity of a writer using a pseudonym.

102. Furthermore, Chapter 3, Article 3 FPA and Chapter 2, Article 3 FSA impose an obligation on everyone involved in production or publication of articles, TV programmes, etc., not to reveal the name or identity – or facts that may lead to such a revelation – of any writers or messengers who wish to remain anonymous.[89] Failure

---

86. To sum this up: Where books (or other non-periodical printing matters) are concerned, only if the author or editor has been identified on the publication by name, or by means of a pseudonym or pen-name known generally to refer to a particular person, or if a person has acknowledged in a written statement that he is the author or editor, or has voluntarily made such a declaration before a court of law during the case, may the question of whether he is liable be considered during the procedure.
87. A new example of this occurred in January 2014, when the Chancellor of Justice decided not to conduct any investigation into which individual policemen or officers who had in 2013 provided the daily newspaper *Dagens Nyheter* with information on police data files dealing only and exclusively with the roma (gypsy) population. At the same time, some earlier attempts to conduct such investigations were criticized.
88. As mentioned below in fn. 120, a partial change may now be brought about, should the proposal in SOU 2013:79 come to be enacted.
89. For a rather recent case, *see* NJA 2012 p. 342, which also indicates that in situations where it might be doubtful whether the informant has accepted that his identity may be revealed (i.e., when the person who is otherwise legally responsible claims this to be the case), the presumption is that this has never happened. Another very interesting case is NJA 2015 p. 298, dealing with the seizure of the

to obey these rules may lead to a prison sentence for as long as a year (Chapter 3, Article 7 FPA and Chapter 2, Article7 FSA). And the anonymity for those persons concerned is protected, also in trials concerning abuses of freedom of speech (Chapter 3, Article 2 FPA and Chapter 2, Article 2 FSA), since it may not be revealed or disclosed even there.[90] However, also here certain exceptions occur, either if the previously anonymous person will accept that his identity may be revealed or in relation to some special crimes, as follows from Chapter 3, Article 4 section 1, p. 1 FPA and Chapter 2, Article 4, section 1, p. 1 FSA.

USB-memory card in a camera belonging to an associate of the daily Dagens Nyheter, who had, during the hunt of a submarine in the archipelago of Stockholm in October 2014, been in a boat inside the military protected zone at a naval regiment, where trespassing and photographing was forbidden. The military police, supported by a prosecutor, seized the memory card with photos taken for the newspaper, a seizure that was approved by the Court of Appeal. However, the Supreme Court concluded, explicitly invoking IG 11:14, that the applicable law according to which seizure was allowed, violated the constititutional Freedom of Press Act (Tryckfrihetsförordningen (TF)), in particular the right for informants to spread facts to the media. Thus, the seizure was annuled in a case that is interesting both because of the very clearly exercised judicial review, where the Supreme Court preferred to prioritize the superior constitution rather than trying to solve the problem through some orthodox interpretative operation and because it shows that judicial review has a role also in issues related to national security. Though somewhat different, the more recent judgment NJA 2024 p. 618 points in the same direction.

90. At the same time, it should perhaps be underlined that no writer or journalist may urge any publisher or editor to publish something on condition of anonymity. The book editor or publisher of a newspaper may of course decide what to publish and by whom. The obligation of silence in relation to messengers is thus more unconditional in its nature.

Chapter 3. Journalists' Liability

§1. General Information on the Liability System

103. The rules on responsibility are different for periodicals compared to non-periodicals; in the first category, the responsible editor at the time when the periodical was published (the criteria of whom are determined in Chapter 5) is normally responsible under Chapter 8, Article 1. This means in practice that if a case is brought against a periodical, the responsible editor (*ansvarig utgivare*) will appear before the court and try to defend the actions of the paper.[91] The editor is normally appointed by the owner, who may of course also decide to replace him. But as long as he holds that position, the editor is considered to have the main responsibility for and also to be deciding on its content, according to FPA Chapter 5, Article 4 nd Chapter 8, Article 2. This also means that in reality, a journalist is very rarely held responsible for what is published in a newspaper, which fits well with the fact that the position of the journalist is as such quite informal in Sweden. While special schools of journalism do of course exist, the exercise of this profession does not require any special licence or education. Thus, anyone who may want to call himself a journalist is free to do so.[92]

104. However, should such an editor not have been properly appointed, the liability will pass over to the owner of the paper,[93] Chapter 8, Article 3, and if his identity is also not established, it will then pass over to the printer, according to Chapter 8, Article 4 FPA. In case the periodical does not properly reveal where it was printed, the responsibility will, as a last step, pass over to the disseminator, under Chapter 8, Article 4 FPA.

105. For non-periodicals, i.e., books, on the other hand, the liability lies primarily with the author under Chapter 8, Article 6, unless he has decided to remain anonymous in accordance with Chapter 3, Articles 1–2 or if it is otherwise clear that the matter has been published without his consent or if his name or pseudonym appears in the book against his will. In that case, liability will pass to the editor, Chapter 8, Article 7, who may however also avoid responsibility in certain peculiar situations,[94] in which cases the publisher will be liable under Chapter 8, Article 8 FPA. If a publisher may not be identified, liability will pass to the printer and ultimately to the disseminator under Chapter 8, Article 9109.

106. In any case, once a responsible person is identified, criminal proceedings (or sometimes tort proceedings) will start under a court in accordance with Chapter 12 FPA (*see also* Chapter 10, Article 1 FSA). The Chancellor of Justice or someone

91. Normally, of course, he is then assisted by a professional lawyer.
92. The same is true for bloggers, who are also totally unregulated (although criminal rules on e.g., libel do of course also apply to them).
93. Who is under Ch. 5, Art. 1 responsible for appointing the editor.
94. In fact, not all books have an editor, which means that the legal importance of this particular article is not always very high.

whom he has appointed is normally the prosecutor on behalf of the State, though in libel cases, it is more usual that persons who feel badly wounded will bring actions to the court themselves.[95] Actions will be heard by a district court with a special competence in that kind of case, Chapter 12, Article 2. In all cases which involve a question of liability under penal law, the question of whether an offence has been committed shall be tried by a jury of nine members, who will establish that an offence has taken place by a majority of six votes to three. However, if the jury finds that no offence has been committed, the defendant shall be acquitted. If the jury on the other hand finds that an offence has been committed, the question shall be examined also by the court, but if the opinion of the court differs from that of the jury, the court is still entitled to acquit the defendant or apply a penal provision carrying a milder sanction than the one applied by the jury. A superior court to which the judgment of a district court has been referred on appeal is no more entitled than the district court to overturn the jury's verdict.

107. This is in fact the only situation in Swedish law where a jury sits.[96] The existence of this jury undoubtedly gives the defendant in freedom of press cases a strong legal position in the trial. Therefore, the jury system is indeed an important part of this particular area of Swedish law, under FPA as well as FSA.

I. Sanctions: The Liability System

108. This may now be further clarified and explained. Gradually, ever since the 'renewed' FPA was enacted in 1812, the insight has grown among lawyers and politicians alike, as well as in the public debate, that the widespread constitutional protection of freedom of speech guaranteed by FPA (and later also by FSA), with absence of censorship and a special procedure in order to establish whether any limits were passed while this freedom was used, should not mean or lead to a legal 'free zone', where any kind of criminal acts may be conducted in certain media under the pretext of free debate and the forming of opinions in societal matters.

95. In fact, when the Chancellor of Justice brings such a case to court, this is a controversial exception. Since 1990, it has only happened three times, both times concerning the daily Expressen. In 1990, the paper was accused of slandering the whole sports movement, having written on 'fixed' matches and ice hockey players being paid to lose and in 2006 the Chancellor acted on behalf of a well-known actor, who was portrayed as residing in a rehab clinic. Though his problems with alcohol and drugs were known, the article was incorrect. The paper was acquitted in the first case, but not the second time.After that, a writer accusing of libel after naming a journalist for sexual abuse related to Metoo was sentenced in 2019. – In 2014, the possibility for the Chancellor of Justice to prosecute on behalf of persons who have been falsely identified as criminals by the webpage Lexbase was being discussed and examined but no change took place. In 2012, on the other hand, the Chancellor quite controversially decided not to bring legal actions against the producer and director of the movie 'Call girl' on behalf of the family of the late Prime Minister Olof Palme, who was in the movie depicted as having a sexual relation with a very young girl.

96. Concerning appointment of the jury and similar issues, *see* Ch. 12, Arts 7–19.

109. The legal technique through which some very important restrictions have then been achieved – which was first presented in the FPA of 1949 – is to enumerate certain crimes, mentioned in the Penal Code,[97] and declare that these are to be considered criminal acts, although or also when they are committed through the use of some constitutionally protected media. As a consequence, in order to add or enact new rules in this area, a constitutional change, requiring two identical parliamentary decisions before and after a general election,[98] is necessary, while the *removal* of a crime from the list may take place through a normal legislative act, since a 'decriminalization' will also mean that the commitment of any such act will never amount to a breach of FPA or FSA.

110. This may be illustrated by the crime illegal threat (*olaga hot*), FPA Chapter 7, Article 2, which was added to the list of punishable crimes in 2002, following a trial in which representatives of the journal Aftonbladet were accused of having committed that crime, having published, in 1998, photos of heavily armed neo-nazis posing outside the homes of a high police officer and the well-known Greek-Swedish journalist Alexandra Pascalidou. The alleged crime was at that time not included in the list in Chapter 7 FPA, which led to the result that the – anonymous – informant who had handed the material over to the journal was protected. Since the journal and its journalists were not themselves involved in the alleged attack, they were not guilty of any crime, which meant that in fact no one was held legally responsible.[99] However, the two persons affected or threatened felt violated by the situation and the reported threat against them and brought their case to the ECtHR, claiming that the lack of applicable legal rules amounted to a violation of their privacy (Article 8 ECHR).[100] In Strasbourg, a compromise was reached between them and the Swedish state and subsequently, in line with this, FPA was changed in order to include also this criminal action.

111. These criminal rules or catalogue(s) of crimes are to be found in Chapter 7, Articles 2–20 FPA and, through a simple reference to the former, also in Chapter 5, Article 1 FSA. And the legal responsibility, then, is borne by the person who is, according to the different situation at hand, to be considered being responsible according to the rules in Chapter 8 FPA and Chapter 6 FSA presented above, regardless of his or her actual criminal intent or even knowledge of what has been printed or uttered. In other words, this is a kind of strict, individual responsibility for the person who is legally designated to be in that position.

112. The catalogue of crimes presented in Chapter 7, Articles 2–20 FPA includes some twenty criminal acts, of which some are undoubtedly more frequent and realistic than others, that have probably not occurred since the nineteenth century. Slander or libel, Chapter 7, Article 3 FPA is by far the most frequent one and this is also

97. The current Penal Code, Brottsbalken, was enacted in 1964, but has since then of course been changed many times. On some occasions, such changes do also require changes in FPA.
98. *See* IG Ch. 8, Arts 14–17.
99. NJA 1999 p. 275.
100. 53970/00, *Pascalidou et al v. Sweden*, dismissed 11 Feb. 2003 (after which Sweden paid compensation).

the one that is most often – in fact normally – brought to a court by an individual who feels offended.[101] However, also insult,[102] incitement to hatred against certain groups or just against the societal order (i.e., *instigation to rebellion*), espionage,[103] disclosures of certain kind of secret or otherwise classified material, depiction of violence[104] and different kinds of threats against different kinds of persons in various situations are also 'real', important crimes that are from time to time brought to the courts. Another kind of rules – of which some are very old – relate to wartime situations and other cases of emergency, which may explain why they are very rarely applied. In 2022, a new and controversial crime was added in Chapter 7, Article 14 FPA, namely the so-called foreign espionage ('utlandsspioneri'), aiming at disclosure of information that may threaten Sweden's cooperation with other states or international organizations. Such disclosure shall however not be considered illegal if it is objectively justified, but no one really knows what that means.

II. The Procedural System

113. In these cases, then, when a crime is suspected, according to Chapter 9, Article 2 FPA, only the Chancellor of Justice, representing the government,[105] may

101. According to rules in the Penal Code (Ch. 5, Art. 5), a public prosecutor may only bring such a case to a court when this is justified by a certain public interest. Now, according to Ch. 9, Art. 2 FPA only the Chancellor of Justice, representing the government, may prosecute in cases concerning violations of FPA (which said rule basically applies also concerning FSA, according to Ch. 7, Art. 1 of that act), but the said limitation then also applies to him, which explains the high frequency of 'private prosecutors' here. – It may also be noted in this respect that companies and other legal persons may never sue anyone for libel or slander. The crime of slander or libel against individuals may, however, be committed even though the circumstances and facts reported are (likely to be) true, should they be detrimental to the reputation of an individual without their publication being necessary or otherwise justified. This was established e.g., by the Stockholm City Court in a controversial case in 1990 concerning the alleged drug consumption of former tennis star Björn Borg.
102. Needless to say, neither procedures concerning this alleged 'crime' is normally initiated by a public prosecutor.
103. Here, we may note that in order for such a crime to be established, real and concrete intent to provide services or favours to another country must be proven (FPA Ch. 7, Art. 4 p. 3). This rule was changed and this requirement laid down in 1976, due to a highly controversial case in 1973–1974 where two young, well-known radical journalists were sentenced to prison for espionage having written critical articles revealing the activities of Swedish military intelligence (the so-called *IB* affair). During the trial against them, they tried in vain to invoke FPA, which would have offered them a much better position. Thus, today they would have been protected by FPA, the editor would have been held responsible and the very radical and critical intent of the articles would have led to the assumption that no real espionage had in fact taken place, since their real purpose was to stir a political debate.
104. This is in fact the only one of the crimes mentioned that has its own, special category within the FSA, due to the technical differences between the different media; *see* Ch. 5, Art. 1, s. 2 FSA.
105. According to Ch. 9, Art. 1 FPA and Ch. 7, Art. 1 FSA, the Chancellor of Justices has a general, supervisory role here, representing the state. He may thus be described as a watchdog against abuses of the freedom of speech, but must be careful himself not to abuse that position. – In 2013, a Jubilee book, celebrating the tri-centennial anniversary of the Chancellor of Justice has been published; *see* Justitiekanslern 300 år, Uppsala (Iustus) 2013.

prosecute in cases concerning violations of FPA (which basically applies also concerning FSA, although with certain exceptions, according to Chapter 7, Article 1 of that act). However, libel and insult cases are, as mentioned above, normally initiated by private parties who feel offended, which follows from rules in the Penal Code indicating that this is the normal route to be followed in such cases.[106] On the other hand, certain crimes (e.g., espionage and other similar actions against the state) may only be prosecuted once the government has allowed the Chancellor of Justice to go ahead with this (FPA Chapter 9, Article 2).

114. A public prosecution should be brought within six months (newspaper) or a year (book) from the date of publication.[107] Should the court find that a crime has occurred, the sentences will normally be the same ones as stipulated by the Penal Code, since both FPA and FSA lack their own rules on sentences and punishment. However, the possible confiscation of a book or journal (or a technical copy of a programme) is a special sanction that may be added according to Chapter 7, Article 26 FPA, as well as Chapter 5, Article 6 FSA.

115. A few more words may here be said about the procedure to be followed in cases under FPA and FSA. Such a trial will, like other trials, be initiated in a Court of First Instance (although only some such designated courts do in fact have jurisdiction). Furthermore, detailed procedural rules are laid down in a special law and regulation that will not be dealt with here.[108] We may however note that twenty-four jurors – the requirements of whom are partly described in Chapter 12, Article 10 FPA[109] – should be chosen for each of Sweden's twenty-two regions (*län*), according to FPA Chapter 2, Article 7.[110]

116. If both of the parties agree to it, the trial may be held without a jury, but this is rarely the case since the existence of the jury will always put the defendant in a favourable and somewhat privileged position, as mentioned above. This is a fact since criminal responsibility will only be established should both the qualified majority of the jury (six of nine jurors) and the three professional judges also sitting in the trial find this to be the case.[111] Those quite complicated but interesting rules are found in Chapter 12, Article 4 FPA and Chapter 10, Article 1 FSA. Apart from that, FPA also contains the special, so-called instruction directed both to jurors and

---

106. A reference to this fact is thus made in Ch. 9, Art. 7 FPA. In this kind of cases, the applicant may choose whether to claim criminal and/or civil (i.e., economical) responsibility for the defendant. However, according to Ch. 11, Art. 1 FPA and Ch. 8, Art. 1 FSA, economical responsibility may only occur once a criminal responsibility has been established (or at least seen to exist). In such cases, the responsibility rules are slightly different and will also include owners of newspapers as well as publishers of books, according to Ch. 11, Art. 2 FPA. *See also* Ch. 11, Arts 3–5, concerning so-called mutual responsibility for various persons involved.
107. Chapter 9, Art. 5 FPA.
108. Lag (1991:1559) med föreskrifter på tryckfrihetsförordningens och yttrandefrihetsgrundlagens områden (LTY).
109. We may here for instance note that they are required to be Swedish citizens.
110. In Stockholm, they are in fact as many as thirty-six.
111. However, the issue of individual responsibility (i.e., who is formally responsible for an article, a book or a program) will only be tried, when necessary, by the professional judges.

judges mentioned above, in Chapter 1, Article 10, which more or less directs them to try to acquit the accused party, should that at all be legally possible.

117. In practice, in a trial, the jury will deliver its verdict first. Should this mean an acquittal of the defendant (i.e., if less than six of nine jurors will find him or her guilty), the case is then in reality over, since a higher instance is also bound by the verdict of the jury, whose influence and importance are thus huge. However, should the jury find the defendant guilty, the three professional judges will also have their say – and their judgment, as well as a 'guilty' judgment (but not the acquittal, thus) from the jury, may be appealed to a higher court.

118. One problem with the jury system is that the jurors – i.e., the persons to be found on the list of jurors, from which the jury itself is then picked or selected – do in fact belong to and are nominated by the political parties, which may sometimes bring about very negative results. One such case, *Holm v. Sweden,* even occurred in the ECtHR, which ruled against Sweden in 1993.[112] In that case, the writer of a book, Mr Hansson, had accused Mr Holm of close cooperation with illegal extreme right groups. Holm, an organized 'anti-leftist', then brought a case to the court, accusing Hansson, who was a member of the Social Democrat party and had published his book in a publishing company owned by that party, of libel. Before the trial, Holm protested against members of the jury who were nominated by the Social Democrats and claimed that they were biased, but his arguments were rejected by the (Stockholm City) Court. Due to somewhat unfortunate circumstances – that the court would in fact have been able to prevent – five of nine jurors at the trial were then Social Democrats. When Hansson was acquitted by the jury, Holm brought a case to the ECtHR, which found that a violation of the right to a fair trial in Article 6 of ECHR had taken place.

§2. Defamation and Libel

119. According to Chapter 7, Article 3 FPA, libel or defamation means alleging or accusing someone of being 'blameworthy in his or her way of life', or otherwise communicating 'information liable to expose another to the contempt of others, and, if the person defamed is deceased, the act causes offend to his or her survivors, or might otherwise be considered to violate the sanctity of the grave except, however, in cases in which it is justifiable to communicate information in the matter, having regard to the circumstances, and proof is presented that the information was correct or there were reasonable grounds for the assertion'.[113] There is thus a certain margin for publishing such facts, though it may be seen as somewhat limited.

112. *Holm v. Sweden*, Judgment 25 Nov. 1993, Series No. 279 – A. – For a study of the history of the jury system, *see* Torbjörn Vallinder, Nio edsvurna män – Jury och tryckfrihet i Sverige 1815–2000, Stockholm 2000.
113. A quotation from the official translation is here used.

120. It must be noted that according to Chapter 9, Article 2 FPA only the Chancellor of Justice, representing the government, may prosecute in cases concerning violations of FPA (which said rule basically applies also concerning FSA, according to Chapter 7, Article 1 of that act), but such cases may only be brought to court when this is justified by a certain public interest.[114] This is the reason for the high frequency of 'private prosecutors' here, concerning libel and defamation. Still, this might be changed in 2015, due to a minor change in the Penal Code making this crime easier for a public prosecutor to enforce (which is due to the alarmingly increased rate of slander and libel at the internet, directed not least against minors).[115] It may also be noted in this respect that companies and other legal persons may never sue anyone for libel or slander.

114. This requirement has caused controversy e.g., when the Chancellor of Justice has prosecuted on behalf of a well-known actor who was falsely said to be under treatment for alcoholism at a rehab clinic. It is far from clear what this actually means.

115. *See* prop 2013/14:47.

Chapter 4. Right to Reply

121. No automatic right to reply for persons who feel that they have been slandered or libelled by media is prescribed by law. What does exist, however, according to Chapter 7, Article 25, section 2 FPA, is the possibility for the court in libel trials where the defendant is convicted – provided that the defendant is a periodical – to order, on request, that the verdict shall be inserted in the periodical. For radio and TV programmes, a similar possibility exists to have the verdict mentioned or referred to in a programme; *see* FSA Chapter 5, Article 7. Furthermore, simple corrections of erroneous facts are to be made in radio and TV programmes whenever justified, as follows from Chapter 5, Article 4 of the law on radio and TV. It may also be mentioned that according to the tort law, *Skadeståndslagen* (1972:207), Chapter 5, Article 6, section 2, anyone who is held responsible for libel, in a criminal or civil case, may – due to the circumstances of the case – be ordered by the court to pay for the printing of the judgment.[116]

122. Also, the possibility for the quasi-supervisory body of the press (*Pressens Opinionsnämnd,* which has existed since 1969) to condemn unserious or false articles and then oblige newspapers to publish those decisions may be mentioned here.

116. *See* most recently the Judgment of the Supreme Court of 28 Feb. 2014, case T 1427-12 (NJA 2014 p. 94).

Chapter 5. Access to Public Information

§1. Public Documents and Meetings

123. The rules on access to documents were originally, in 1766 and the IG of 1809, formulated as a right to *print* public documents (i.e., in newspapers, primarily). However, since this would not be possible if these documents were not accessible for publishing in the first place, the obligation for public authorities to hand over documents to interested parties was regulated. All of this was – and is still – basically seen as a means for the press (and thus the public) to check and supervise the public administration, in order to promote democracy and rule of law and thus prevent corruption and other forms of abuse of power.

124. Today, the rules on access to documents are to be found in Chapter 2 FPA and the new law on Transparency and Secrecy of 2009 (Offentlighets- och Sekretesslagen (OSL), 2009:400). The point of departure here is still that public documents are accessible for anyone who wishes to study them[117] and that they should be handed over from the public authority to the one who wants to see them without any undue delay; as a sign of this, that person does not have to reveal his name or identity, unless the establishment of a person's identity may be decisive for the determination of the legal possibility to hand the document(s) over (Chapter 2, Article 14, section 3 FPA). Also, documents that are from the beginning 'private' as to their nature may be considered public once they have been handed over to a public authority; at least, this is the presumption and the normal routine.[118]

125. However, certain limitations of this general right to information do of course exist.[119] In fact, the interests in the name of which it may be limited are enumerated in Chapter 2, Article 2 FPA. Here, important national political and economical interests are mentioned, as well as certain individual or personal interests

117. This is also strongly underlined in Ch. 2, Art. 1 FPA.

118. *See* the case RÅ 1998 ref. 42 from the Supreme Administrative Court, where exactly this happened concerning the so-called bible of the Scientology Church, which was allegedly secret and accessible only for members of that 'religious' community. In January 2014, a student of journalism as a practical joke sent his private pet animal, a turtle, to a public authority in order to have it registered as 'public', but the request was denied. – Needless to say, perhaps, these rules may come into conflict with rules in other EU Member States and with EU law itself (although Swedish and Finnish EU membership since 1995 has actually made the Union somewhat more transparent). Recently, the Government has proposed certain new limitations of access to documents in different forms of international cooperation; *see* prop 2012/13:192.

119. The Swedish rules may also be in conflict with certain parts of EU law, notably perhaps the directive 95/46 on protection for individuals in relation to certain personal information (transformed into Swedish law by the so-called *Personuppgiftslagen, PuL*, 1998:204). In the case NJA 2001 p. 409, the Supreme Court clearly favourized and gave priority to FPA in such a situation of conflict (referring also to Arts 8 and 10 of ECHR). *See also* the case C-101/01, Lindquist, ECR 2003 I p. 12971 from ECJ on other aspects of this sometimes rather complicated issue. – In the discussion on the above-mentioned webpage Lexbase, its critics also argued that its activities violated PuL, which was seen as a possible reason for changing FSA Ch. 1, Art. 9. This was somewhat ironic and could even be seen as a sign of moral panic, since all previous discussions, during its fifteen years of existence, have indicated that PuL and the directive 95/46 are a kind of 'necessary evil' that will,

(and, oddly enough, 'the interest of preserving a certain species of animal or vegetable').[120] The more detailed criteria on how public bodies are to deal with requests for documents are then laid down in the new law of 2009 (which replaced an old, similar one from 1980). It is also important to keep in mind that this right applies only in relation to public agencies, but not in relation to NGO's or private companies, for example.[121]

§2. Court Hearings and Documents

126. What has been said above is applicable also to court hearings and documents in court cases. According to IG Chapter 2, Article 11, court proceedings are public, though limitations are possible by law according to Chapter 2, Article 20, section 1, p. 4. In practice, courts do often declare that certain proceedings or sessions are to be held behind closed doors, according to rules in the law on Transparency and Secrecy.

---

when any conflict occurs, have to bow for the principle of transparency, with its deep historical roots (as shown also by the Supreme Court in 2001).

120. Chapter 2, Art. 2, s. 1 p. 7 FPA.

121. It may be noted here that the Royal Court has not been considered as a public body in the jurisprudence applying and interpreting these rules; *see* the case RÅ 1999 ref. 48 from the Supreme Administrative Court. On the other hand, companies owned by municipalities are bound by the rules (but not state-owned companies, which may seem somewhat contradictory). A new proposal in 2013, SOU 2013:79 (*Stärkt meddelarskydd för privatanställda i offentligt finansierad verksamhet*) recommends to extend the protection to privately owned companies operating within the school or health care systems.

Chapter 6. Relation with EU

127. Some other aspects of the Swedish regulation mentioned above that have at times been seen, by various legislative committees, e.g., before Sweden joined the EU, as difficult to reconcile with EU law, are the rules on access to documents and freedom for whistleblowers, which have very few equivalents in other EU Member States.[122] Subsequent developments within EU law, such as the sharper rules on access to documents and open administration[123] and, not least, the recognition of the constitutional identity of the Member States, now mentioned, since 2009, in Article 4 section 2 of the Treaty of the European Union, may have reduced those tensions slightly (or even considerably). However, to give an example of the underlying difficulties, the Constitutional Committee of the Parliament (*Konstitutionsutskottet*) in 2012, while exercising its so-called review of subsidiarity in accordance with Article 69 of the Treaty on the functioning of the EU, protested against the use of a regulation as the legal act for new rules on the use of personal data, since the use of a directive for these same rules would give the Member States a greater legal space for action, including a necessary consideration of the national legal context.[124] Here, it may also be mentioned that the Swedish Parliament did, in November 2013, by a controversial move, approve new limitations of the general and widespread access to documents whenever secrecy may be due to international cooperation or asked for by international organizations (including the EU).[125] Many journalists and press organizations have reacted very critically against these changes, the effects of which are yet impossible to assess.

---

122. *See* e.g., KU 1993/94:21, in particular p. 25 ss, as well as prop 1993/94:114.
123. *See* here Art. 41 of the EU Charter of Fundamental Rights.
124. *See* KU 2011/12:25. – It may be mentioned here that the EU directive (2006/24) on Electronic Data Retention has been controversial in Swedish law for a long time. Sweden didn't implement it in due time (i.e., by 15 Sep. 2007), which led to an infringement procedure against Sweden before the ECJ, who found in 2010 that Sweden had violated EU law (Case C-185/09, *Commission v. Sweden*, Judgment 4 Feb. 2010, ECR 2010 I p. 14). Finally, the directive was implemented through a law adopted by the Parliament in March 2012, but before that, the opposition parties had used a rule in IG (Ch. 2, Art. 22) according to which laws that limit fundamental rights may be postponed one year. Since the Advocate General Cruz Villalon delivered a critical opinion on the directive in December 2013 (*see* Joined Cases C-293/12, Digital Rights Ireland and C-594/12, Seitlinger and Others), a renewed debate on the directive and its effects for the personal integrity seems to be emerging; the judgment in those two cases on 8 Apr. 2014 was thus eagerly awaited and the fact that the ECJ declared the directive incompatible with the fundamental rights that form a part of EU law means that the legal status of the directive and the said law within Swedish law is today uncertain. The Minister of Justice has stated that the law remains in force, while the surveilling authority, *Post- och telestyrelsen* (PTS) has made comments pointing in another direction. A rapidly presented official bill (Ds 2014:23) confirmed the legality of the Swedish law, but subsequent proceedings have pointed in another direction.
125. *See* KU 2013/14:6, *Sekretess i det internationella samarbetet*, as well as rskr 2013/14:59, leading to the law 2013:972 containing changes in the Secrecy Law.- If we focus on the so-called Data Retention Directive in relation to personal integrity, we may note that from the CJEU, cases such as Digital Rights Ireland in 2014 have clarified that the directive may violate the protection of personal integrity in Arts 7–8 of the Charter of Fundamental Rights, since it had not determined the grounds for access to the data pertaining to national authorities and its storage. Also the case Tele2 from 2016 should be mentioned. Thus, the integrity of EU-citizens has clearly been strengthened since the Charter entered into force.

128. However, so far the ECJ has not had the opportunity to review or interpret FPA or FSA, at least not from any of those points of view. Needless to say, in such a procedure, the Swedish government would strongly defend Swedish particularities and traditions in this area, but here, it is an open question whether many other Member States would actually support the Swedish position.

The same goes for the case Schrems ('Facebook'), where CJEU reviewed and annulled a previous decision from the Commission stating that USA had a sufficient protection for personal data for information to be sent there. And in Google Spain from 2014, where Google was ordered to remove information on a bankruptcy that was nine years old, Arts 7–8 in the Charter were allowed clear horizontal effect ('so-called Drittwirkung'). Thus, a connection between Drittwirkung and personal integrity is now acknowledged within EU law.

Chapter 7. Broadcasting Authority and Press Council

129. The public authority responsible for granting permissions or licences to direct TV programmes is the Swedish Broadcasting Authority, *Mediemyndigheten*. However, the right to direct programmes may also be granted by the government. In both cases, a right to appeal against the decision before a court is guaranteed by FSA Chapter 3, Article 7.

130. The Swedish Broadcasting Commission, *Granskningsnämnden för radio och TV*, is a separate decision-making body within the Swedish Broadcasting Authority that monitors whether the content of radio and television programmes adheres to the broadcasting regulations. This authority also controls that the broadcasting companies follow the conditions in their licences.[126]

131. In the area covered by FPA, a similar 'semi-supervisory' body (*Pressens Opinionsnämnd*, 'Press Council') has existed since 1969 (and originally in fact since 1916). This is however not regulated by law and it has few, if any, formal powers. Still, it may condemn unserious or false articles and newspapers may then be obliged to publish those decisions. It has published rules and principles for good ethical behaviour of the Press. Of its no less than eighteen members, who work in two chambers, the president is normally a judge. The same goes for the three vice presidents. It must however be noted that this whole activity is privately financed and only applicable to the media companies that have signed a special agreement to follow it, in order to enforce a kind of self-regulatory system that is in a way working well, since the Swedish Press in general has fairly good ethics. The Press Council thus has no formal powers and the same goes for the special Press Ombudsman. Material published on the internet may be reviewed by the Press Council or the Ombudsman in the same way as other press material, provided that the publisher has joined the system.

126. For further information on the activities of this body, *see* its webpage http://mediemyndigheten.se.

Part III. Regulation of Audiovisual Media (Broadcasting)

Chapter 1. Public Service Broadcasting

§1. The Concept and Mission of Public Service Broadcasting

132. Basically, the task of public service can be said to consist in devoting more time and space to information, debates, serious journalism, minority language programmes and culture than the other, commercial channels (and consequently less time to entertainment). This is however not regulated by law, but in an agreement between the state and the formally independent companies Sveriges Radio, SR, Utbildningsradion, UR, and Sveriges Television, SVT. For the period 2014–2019, the main conditions for their activities were laid down in a bill from 2013.[127] Here, it was stated that the system with licence fees should continue and that the radio system should be gradually digitalized.

§2. The Organization of Public Service Broadcasting

133. Only the state-owned companies Sveriges Radio and Sveriges Television are counted as public service companies, together with their branch office *Utbildningsradion* (Radio for education, UR). These so-called *public service companies* are ordered to provide the public or the people as a whole with impartial, independent and objective TV and radio programme material. Among the current rules on public service, we may note that they must announce any new kind of (technical) services (mainly on TV) to the government. The radio and TV authority will then give an opinion on whether any new activities are in line with the special public service task and how they will affect the whole media market situation. At the same time, it must be stressed that those companies are financed by licence fees, which all TV owners have to pay (circa SEK 2000 per year) and are organizationally totally independent of the government.

127. Prop 2012/13:164, Bildning och tillgänglighet – radio och TV i allmänhetens tjänst 2014-2019.

134. Since 1997, these companies – that are managed as companies under the Swedish company law – are governed and owned by a special trust (*Förvaltningsstiftelsen för Sveriges Radio AB, Sveriges Television AB och Sveriges Utbildningsradio AB*), which has a board with thirteen members, all of whom are nominated by the political parties in Parliament and formally appointed by the government. The chairman is elected for four years and the others all for eight years. The boards and the managing directors are then appointed at annual shareholders' meetings.

§3. THE FINANCING OF PUBLIC SERVICE BROADCASTING

135. Apart from the licence fees, which are regulated by a special law from 1989,[128] the PSB companies may gain some money by allowing private companies to sponsor certain programmes. Sponsoring is thus allowed here, with the restrictions explained below, but not commercial advertising.

128. Lagen (1989:41) om finansiering av radio och TV i allmänhetens tjänst. Here, it may be mentioned that according to a recent, quite surprising judgment of the Supreme Administrative Court (Case 7368-13, 13 Jun. 2014), viewers who watch TV 'only' from internet-connected computers do not have to pay this license.

Chapter 2. Private Broadcasting

§1. Different Categories of Private Broadcasters

136. As mentioned above, the concentration of media in the hands of a few owners is actually very high in Sweden and it seems to be a fact that the rather peculiar constitutional regulation of the media sector does in fact contribute to this. The two main actors that are influential in all or at least many areas (TV, radio, internet, press) are Bonniers, an old family empire based in Stockholm, and MTG (Modern Times Group), another Swedish family group (built by the late Jan Stenbeck but now controlled by other investors). However, in sheer terms, also the Swedish state and the Norwegian media group Schibsted are very big, though the state is active only in TV and radio and Schibsted mainly in the daily press.[129] Apart from these actors, also the German SBS, working in TV and radio, is an important operator.

137. In the TV sector, the four leading companies Sveriges Television (SVT, public service), TV 4 (Bonniers), MTG and SBS own the TV stations that dominate the market, with a total of 90% of all viewing.[130] Individually, of these actors, SVT has 36.6% and TV 428.9%. Here, a clear concentration of ownership in a few hands is thus visible. While the public service channels show more programmes devoted to information and facts than ever, the tendency in the commercial channels is the opposite.

138. In the radio sector, apart from the public service company, *Sveriges Radio (SR)*, financed by public fees in the same way as Sveriges Television, all other radio stations are financed by advertisements. Of these totally 103 private operators, in 2013, the two giants MTG and SBS managed no less than 101. The 103 licences that were then granted are all geographically limited and cover different parts – but together all – of Sweden. All except very few (eight) have been auctioned by the state. They were valid until 1 August 2018, after which, they had to be renewed or sold to other actors. When digitalization happens, in 2022 at the latest, the idea is to organize the radio sector slightly differently, with two networks each covering sixteen available radio channels. Both national and regional transmissions will then be possible, in a total of thirty-four regions. At the local level, local, small radio stations (*närradio*) are very common; it is fairly easy for those stations to get a licence from the public radio and TV authority, as follows from Chapter 12 of the law on radio and TV.

---

129. It also manages some important and profitable sites on the internet, such as 'www.blocket.se', where very many Swedes sell and buy various things.
130. Thus, the dominating channels, are the so-called big five: SVT1 (24.3%), SVT2 (6.7%), TV 3 (MTG, 6.4%), TV 4 (18.9%) and finally Kanal 5 (SBS, 6.1%).

§2. LICENSING REQUIREMENTS

139. Apart from the five basic TV channels SVT 1, SVT 2, TV 4, TV 6 and SVT *Kunskapskanalen*, for which no cable is required, competition in the cable area is basically free. No licence is required to broadcast cable television and IPTV. However, so-called original broadcasts must be registered with the Swedish Broadcasting Authority (Myndigheten för radio och tv). The same also applies to satellite broadcasts.

140. As mentioned above, the public authority responsible for granting permissions to direct TV programmes is the new *Myndigheten för radio och TV*. However, the right to direct programmes may also be granted by the government. In both cases, a right to appeal against the decision before a court is guaranteed by FSA Chapter 3, Article 7. As was also previously mentioned, traditional TV, covering the 'basic channels' mentioned above (which have been digital since 2007 but still transmitted 'on the ground') are the only kind of transmissions that still require a licence. The government decides on this licence or permission for the public service channels and the Public Authority for radio and TV does the same for the commercial channels.

141. One major difference between FPA and FSA, which is in fact not clearly expressed by the wording of FSA and may thus not easily be grasped, is that total freedom of establishment does in fact still not exist in the TV and radio sector.

142. This should perhaps be clarified a little bit more. Concerning TV and radio transmissions, a distinction is made in Chapter 3, Articles 1–2 between transmissions by landline, which are entirely free for anyone to operate,[131] and the right to transmit radio programmes through the digital terrestrial network, which is – given the scarcity of resources involved – regulated in an act of law containing provisions on licensing and conditions on transmission. This is of course particularly important as far as radio and TV programmes are concerned, while other technical recordings may be produced and disseminated by anyone according to Chapter 3, Article 3.[132]

143. Thus, according to Chapter 3, Article 3, section 2 FSA, public authorities must try to ensure that all radio frequencies are used in a way that will most benefit freedom of speech and freedom of information. Also, the legislator must bear this in mind, as stated in Chapter 3, Article 3. TV frequencies are quite limited.[133] And

131. *See* Ch. 3, Art. 1.

132. The text here only talks of Swedish citizens and legal persons, but as follows from Ch. 11, Art. 1, , foreign nationals are normally equated with Swedish citizens under FSA (though differences may be provided in law). – A proposal for some modernizing changes in this act has been made through the bill 2009/10:81.

133. In fact, this problem may get even worse in 2017, should the government advance with plans to reserve certain frequencies and TV networks for the expansion of networks available for mobile phones.

according to Chapter 3, Article 7, any decision not to grant an applicant a permission for transmission of radio or TV programmes may be reviewed by a court.[134] These same rules will also apply to radio and TV programmes that are sent (i.e., coming) from Sweden but then broadcasted or sent (i.e., transmitted) abroad by satellite, as stated in Chapter 1, Article5 FSA.[135] Concerning programmes *sent from abroad but received* in Sweden, FSA is only partially applicable, as follows from its Chapter 1, Article 3. This has to do with the fact that editors or other persons who are normally legally responsible in Sweden will have very limited possibilities to influence the content of such transmissions.[136] It may also be mentioned that according to a decision from the Swedish Broadcasting Commission (Granskningsnämnden för radio och TV) in October 2012, video sections on newspaper websites are to be considered audiovisual media services, since these sections are seen as separate from other content on the webpages (Dec. No. 12/00777-780). The matter has however not been decided by a court and has, as opposed to many other EU Member States, not led to any widespread debate.

144. The public authority responsible for granting permissions to broadcast in the digital terrestrial network, normally for six years, is the new *Myndigheten för radio och TV,* as mentioned above. However, the broadcasting permissions for the public service broadcasting companies are granted by the government, which will then also decide on their duration.[137] In both cases, a right to appeal against the decision before a court is guaranteed by FSA Chapter 3, Article 7.

134. Furthermore, these possible restrictions of the right to transmit TV and radio programs will of course never affect the content of the programs that are lawfully transmitted and the full, sovereign right of the license holder to determine this. This fact may indeed seem very natural, but nevertheless Ch. 1, Arts 1 and 13 FSA underline it very clearly. Still, certain restrictions concerning e.g., the right to commercial advertising may be combined with a license, and these restrictions must then be observed; *see* Ch. 1, Art. 9.

135. *See* the case NJA 2005 p. 884. The same applies for so-called web-based programs, directed and sent by the internet; *see* Ch. 1, Art. 8-9FSA. The mere fact that a server may be located abroad is not decisive in this respect, as shown by the case NJA 2001 p. 445. – However, Ch. 1, Art. 6, s. FSA and the law on radio and TV foresee certain exceptions for radio and TV programs intended to be reviewed abroad, as well as for programs that are sent only in small communities or neighbourhoods consisting of no more than 100 houses.

136. For that same reason, important limitations as to the applicability of FSA occur also in relation to directly transmitted political events or religious services; *see* FSA Ch. 1, Art. 16 for more details.

137. For further details, *see* Ch. 4, Art. 12 in the law on radio and TV . – It may be noted that in the area covered by FPA, a similar 'semi-supervisory' body (*Pressens Opinionsnämnd*) has existed since 1969 (and in its original form since 1916). This is however not regulated by law and has few, if any formal powers, as mentioned above. It may however condemn unserious or false articles and newspapers may then be obliged to publish those decisions. Of its no less than eighteen members, the president is normally a judge. The same goes for the three vice-presidents.

Chapter 3. Programme Standards

§1. Impartiality

145. As mentioned above, no automatic right to reply exists, but the impartiality rule for public service broadcasting companies means, among other things, that a person or party who has been clearly criticized in a programme shall be given the chance to present their view on the issue and that controversial matters may never be treated in a one-sided or biased way.[138]

146. In February 2014, a somewhat heated debate took place concerning a comedian (*Soran Ismail*), who was banned from participating in all programmes sent by the state (public service) TV and radio companies (Sveriges Radio, Sveriges Television) until after the election in September 2014, since he was an outspoken critic of the far-right party *Sverigedemokraterna.* The public service channels are bound by rules on political objectivity, but the supporters of Mr Ismail invoked Chapter 5, Article 1 of the new law on radio and TV in his defence. This rule states that any TV or radio broadcaster must always ensure that the emissions and its activities as a whole are characterized by 'the basic ideas of democracy, the principle of equal value of all persons and the freedom and dignity of the individual'. However, the decision not to allow him space for a limited time, due to the fact that he was not willing to accept well-known rules of objectivity, has also been supported by many commentators.

§2. Cultural Diversity

147. In a survey of a public committee from 2012,[139] the need to protect cultural and linguistic diversity in the TV and radio programmes broadcasted by the PSB companies was sharply underlined. Later, in 2013, the Ministry of Culture repeated this in its bill for PSB activities until 2019.[140] There is currently extensive regulation regarding, e.g., culture, an equality and diversity perspective, minority language, etc., in the public service broadcasting.[141] Meanwhile, Chapter 5, Article 7 of the Radio and TV Act obliges terrestrial TV broadcasters to make sure that more than half of their emission time each year will be devoted to TV programmes with a European origin.

138. These rules on the content may be found at http://www.mrtv.se/en/content-regulation/.
139. SOU 2012:59, Nya villkor för public service.
140. Prop 2012/13:164.
141. *See* SVTs permit (in Swedish) http://www.mrtv.se/Documents/S%c3%a4ndningstillst%c3%a5nd/13-03012%20Regeringsbeslut_Sandningstillstand-SVT.pdf?epslanguage=sv.

§3. Protection of Minors (Indecency and Violence)

148. According to the radio and TV law, Chapter 5, Articles 2–3 (that apply to any kind of TV programmes, linear, on demand or whatever), programmes with detailed and lifelike depictions of violence or pornographic images must come with a warning. Such programmes may not be aired at such a time and in such a way that there is a substantial risk that children may see them, unless this is justifiable for special reasons.

149. The broadcasting permits for terrestrial television contain a regulation on 'the impact of the Media'. The broadcaster shall take into account the impact of radio and television in terms of format, topics and time of transmission. This provision is applied in the evaluation of programmes that contain or deal with subject matter such as violence, sex and drugs, and implies that broadcasting companies should exercise caution. Programmes that could be construed as inciting criminal activity are not permitted. Features that are clearly offensive to either gender are also prohibited, as well as programmes which are offensive to people of an ethnic minority group, religion or sexual orientation. The application of this provision is affected, for example, by whether the programme or feature is satirical or humorous in nature.

150. Also, rules on advertising are stricter in relation to minors, as explained below.

§4. Human Dignity

151. Traditionally, no specific rules on human dignity are to be found in the Swedish constitution or in Swedish law in general. However, respect for individual freedom and human dignity is now mentioned as a general requirement for any broadcasting company, according to Chapter 5, Article 1 of the law on radio and TV. Apart from that, the general rule prohibiting incitement to hatred against certain groups (*hets mot folkgrupp*) in Chapter 16, Article 8 of the Criminal Act also applies to TV emissions (FPA Chapter 7, Article 6, p. 11 and FSA Chapter 5, Article 1).

Chapter 4. Political Broadcasting

§1. Rules on Political Independence of Broadcasters

152. Apart from what is mentioned elsewhere in this text, no further specific rules on independence from political parties exist. The main idea is thus that while PBS are independent, private broadcasters do not have to be so.

§2. Fair Representation in Election Periods

153. There is an obligation of the state radio and TV (public service, i.e., not allowing advertising) to observe strict neutrality during electoral campaigns. Since commercial broadcasting is becoming ever more important in society, the relevance of this legislation may of course be questioned, but here it may be noted that the new radio and TV law of 2010 contains prohibitions against favourization of any certain commercial interests. In the extreme, worst case, a violation of these rules may lead to a loss of the permission to broadcast.[142]

§3. News and Current Affairs Programmes

154. The general rules on impartiality and independence that apply to all programmes also apply here. As explained below, rules on advertising and sponsoring are considerably stricter for these programmes, though.

§4. Political Advertising

155. No rules exist concerning which persons, organizations, classes or groups of persons or of organizations, if any, are expressly forbidden from contributing to political parties. The general rules against bribery and corruption in the penal code will apply should any such crimes be suspected. Those rules have been changed and sharpened in recent years, due to new rules and conventions within the EU and the Council of Europe.

156. No restrictions concerning political campaign activities of civil servants and other public employees exist as such, which is worth noting. This is typically considered a part of the freedom of speech, though it goes without saying that the public confidence in leading civil servants or judges would not survive a strong political bias from any of them.

142. Such a sanction may however only be given by a court, acting with a jury, while the state will then be represented by the Chancellor of Justice. It may also be noted that according to Ch. 4, Art. 10 of this new and rather extensive law, the government may in fact prohibit commercial advertising in any TV channel.

157. No real restrictions seem to exist neither concerning 'official' use of public resources by elected officials during election campaign periods or at other times (e.g., use of broadcasted and printed media or through various means of public transportation), but it may be noted that excessive use of such resources might be considered a misuse of public funds, as shown by criticism towards the former Prime Minister when he used the official governmental airplane for internal party affairs during the preparations for the election campaign in 2002.[143]

158. Measures do exist to protect challenger candidates from the media and communication advantages believed in some countries to favour incumbents, but mainly in the form of the obligation of the state radio and TV (public service, i.e., not allowing advertising) to observe strict neutrality during electoral campaigns.

159. There used to be restrictions on the use of broadcast media in political campaigns, in the form of a voluntary agreement between almost all media companies and networks not to allow pure political advertising (an agreement that did however apply permanently). It is only the state radio and TV, as well as the channel TV 4 (a private TV company with a national concession) that are regulated by law in this respect. This fact does of course increase the importance of the new law on radio and TV of 2010.

143. A similar discussion arose when the Minister of Finance Mr Ringholm in 2004 used the government's plane in order to fly back from a match at the European Championship in Football in Portugal to a Trade Union Conference. The question whether national legislation does provide for enforcement action/penalties against corrupt practices committed abroad (*outside* national jurisdiction) is a general issue related to penal law. It may be mentioned that there is a special rule in this respect in Ch. 19, Art. 13 of the Penal Code (Brottsbalken).

Chapter 5. Advertising Rules

160. Also, when talking of and analysing the legal situation concerning commercial advertising, the particular Swedish regulation may cause certain problems.[144] As mentioned above, FPA (as well as FSA) does not protect commercial advertising as such, but this is only partly true, since advertising that may also contain parts of opinions or contribute to the forming of opinions is in fact protected,[145] as has been shown a number of times in the jurisprudence of Swedish courts.[146] But for any kind of purely commercial advertising, which is intended only to sell certain products or favours, the law on marketing (Marknadsföringslagen) will apply, regardless of where it has been published or displayed.

161. This law has existed, in different forms, since the 1970s. It is supervised by a special Market court, which may, among other things, control that companies and other commercial operators will not use unjust or unfair methods in their marketing, in line not least with the EU Directive 2005/29.[147] In order to maintain a high standard in the field of advertising and to protect the interests of the Swedish consumers, the Court may use economic sanctions as well as injunctions and prohibitions on some kind of advertising, together with other administrative measures. Cases may be brought to the court by the Consumer Ombudsman, by individuals or groups of consumers or by other commercial operators, who feel wounded by the activities of some company (*see* Articles 47–53 of the law).

162. In order to illustrate the legal difficulties in this area, the case *Gourmet* may be mentioned. Here, a periodical called Gourmet and specializing in articles on food and wine had published some outspoken commercial advertising for wines, which the consumers' ombudsman wanted to put an end to (invoking not least FPA Chapter 1, Article 9, p. 1). The city court of Stockholm asked for a preliminary ruling from ECJ, which found the Swedish prohibition against this kind of advertisement far-reaching and problematic.[148] Both the city court and the special Market Court (Marknadsdomstolen) then found it impossible to maintain the prohibition.[149]

---

144. One such problem, that will however not be dealt with further here, is the lack of legal remedies for companies and other legal persons who feel that they have been subject to libel or slander (something that may of course cause them great financial harm, should the allegations be true or not). This is of course mainly due to shortcomings or peculiarities in the Penal Code, that have its roots in a case from 1904 (NJA 1904 p. 483). It may undoubtedly seem strange that the issue has not been reviewed afterwards.
145. *See* e.g., prop 1994/95:123 p. 84 s, as well as prop 2007/08:115 p. 111 s.
146. *See* e.g., NJA 1975 p. 589 and 1977 p. 751, as well as RÅ 2010 p. 115 (I–II). – The latter case concerned advertisements for betting and lotteries. This is of course a commercial activity, but since the issue of whether this should be reserved for state-owned or state-controlled companies or whether freedom of establishment and free movement of services should prevail (thus giving foreign companies a fair share of the market) has been contested, the advertisements were considered as also taking part of the societal debate, and thus worthy of the protection of the FPA.
147. In 2015, this was replaced bya new Patent and Market Court, that also deals with patents, i.e., a part of the Intellectual Property law.
148. C-405/98, Gourmet, ECR 2001 I p. 1795.
149. MDA 2003:5.

163. On all those issues mentioned here, it may be noted that the two European courts and perhaps in particular ECJ may take a slightly different approach, should they get the chance. While the ECtHR has a clear focus on freedom of speech (Article 10 ECHR) as a human right, though not always treating these matters in ways that are identical to the ones taken by Swedish lawyers,[150] the ECJ here tends to focus also on the so-called four freedoms and notably the free movement of services. It may be noted, however, that ECJ has allowed limitations of the commercial advertising for tobacco, in a way that seems consistent with FPA, Chapter 1, Article 12, p. 2.[151] Both courts also basically seem to share the Swedish view that commercial advertising in general – or 'commercial speech' as it is sometimes also called – may well deserve protection, but not to the same extent as other forms of messages.[152]

§1. Various Forms of Commercial Communications

164. The main rules concerning definitions of advertising, sponsorship and product placement are to be found in Chapters 6 and 7 (for TV) and 15 (radio) of the law on radio and TV from 2010, which was in fact enacted, replacing an older law from 1996, in order to implement the audiovisual services directive 2007/65 and subsequent modifications in directive 2010/13 into Swedish law. The first of those directives should have been implemented by December 2009, so Sweden was obviously a bit slow here. It should thus be assumed that Sweden does meet the requirement in those directives, but it must be noted that in 2013, the EU Commission initiated an infringement case against Sweden. The Swedish government gave its critical opinion on 21 March 2014, but later succumbed to the EU opinion. Some of the contested matters related to areas where Sweden claims that FSA makes other regulations than the existing ones impossible, such as access for disabled persons to pay-TV and the possibilities for TV emissions from other Member States to reach Swedish viewers. Other contested items concern the journalistic independence of commercial TV channels in relation to sponsoring and product placement, where the law on radio and TV may be seen as harsh, as explained below, and insufficient efforts of Sweden to promote European TV-productions involving also other Member States.

165. Sponsoring is allowed, as mentioned above, but according to Chapter 7, Article 1, not for news programmes. Product placement is allowed in movies, TV series, sport and entertainment programmes, according to Chapter 6, Article 2 of the law on radio and TV, but not for alcohol, tobacco or medicines (pharmaceuticals) and not at all in children's programmes (i.e., programmes for viewers younger than

150. Here, we may once again refer to the case on the privacy of Princess Caroline of Monaco, which was considered to have been violated when she had been photographed in a supermarket (*Caroline von Hannover v. Germany,* Judgment 24 Jun. 2004, 59320/00). This situation would most likely have been considered differently by a Swedish court.

151. *See* C-380/03, *Germany v. Parliament and Council*, ECR 2006 I p. 11573.

152. *See* from ECtHR e.g., *VGT v. Switzerland,* Appl.no. 24699/94, Judgment 28 Jun. 2001 and from ECJ C-71/02, Karner, ECR 2004 I p. 3025.

12 years of age). However, such programmes may never benefit specific commercial interests in an inappropriate way (Chapter 6, Article 3 and Chapter 5, Article 5). In radio emissions, the same rules will apply and it may also be noted that special jingles or tunes must be heard before and after advertisements, in order to separate those parts of the programmes from the other content (Chapter 15, Article 1).

§2. Restrictions on Content

166. Apart from what has been said above, it may also be mentioned that commercial advertising for alcohol and tobacco is also forbidden by rules in a law on alcohol (2010:1622), Chapter 7, Article 3, and the law on tobacco (1993:581), Article 14. These rules are lawful and constitutional according to FPA Chapter 1, Article 12, p. 1 and FSA Chapter 1, Article 18.

§3. Time and Frequency Restrictions

167. In TV, advertisements may be broadcast for a maximum of twelve minutes every hour (radio and TV law, Chapter 8, Article 1).[153] They may never be shorter than one minute at a time, except in live sports shows (Chapter 8, Article 2). Advertisements are never allowed in religious sermons or in programmes sent mainly to children. A special signature must announce that advertisements are about to begin (Chapter 8, Article 4). Also, in radio programmes, special jingles or tunes must be heard before and after advertisements, in order to separate those parts of the programmes from the other content, as mentioned above. Chapter 6 of the Radio and TV Act contains rules on product placement, which is basically forbidden but with some exceptions, notably for movies, TV serials, sport shows and entertainment. It is never allowed in programmes aimed at minors (i.e., younger than 12 years) or when it comes to alcohol, tobacco and pharmaceuticals and may never favourize certain commercial interests. When it occurs, information on this must occur at the beginning and end of the programme, and also when it re-commences after a commercial break.

153. Still, special programs devoted entirely to the selling of certain products (e.g., 'TV shop') are allowed, provided that they will last for at least fifteen minutes.

Chapter 6. Right to Information

§1. Access to Major Events

168. Finally, it may be noted that in Sweden, the sole right for certain private TV companies to transmit and broadcast big sporting events has recently been much discussed. Here, it seems clear that EU law does allow national rules that may impose an obligation on those private companies to share at least parts of the content with state-owned companies or with TV channels that are available to huge parts of the population, without undue costs.[154] This view looks likely to prevail in Sweden as well and rules aiming at such a result do exist in Chapter 5, Articles 9–10 of the law on radio and TV.

169. As far as the Olympic Games are concerned, the International Olympic Committee decided in 2009 that the emission rights should no longer be reserved for public service companies. In Sweden, the satellite channel Viasat bought the rights to both the winter Olympic Games in 2014 and the summer Olympic Games in Rio de Janeiro in 2016, for an alleged sum of SEK 250,000,000. The radio and TV authority then issued in 2013 a list of events that must be shown in channels that are available to huge parts (i.e., 80%) of the population, which does in reality mean SVT 1, SVT 2, TV 4 and TV 6 (and then indirectly also TV 3 and perhaps TV 5). Since Viasat is a part of the MTG group, which owns TV 3 and 6, as well as the smaller TV 10, all emissions from the Sotji games were shown in these channels, as well as in Viasat's satellite programmes. The list of events does, besides important sporting events, also include popular programmes such as the Eurovision Song Contest.

154. C-283/11, Sky Österreich GmbH, ECR 2013:28.

Chapter 7. Access to Networks

§1. Must Carry Rules

170. The conditions that may be imposed on TV companies and networks in order for them to be granted licences to broadcast are enumerated in Chapter 4, Articles 8–11 of the radio and TV law. The longest and most important rule is Chapter 4, Article 9, which states that a license to broadcast may be given with certain obligations e.g., to broadcast in the whole country or certain parts of it, to broadcast for a minimum time, using special techniques (also suited for disabled persons), considering the need for pluralism and diversity of programmes, to publish messages of importance for the public free of cost and to respect the privacy of individuals. No requirement as such is made for the number of channels of each company. Concerning the requirement of 'must carry rules' in some EU directives, Chapters 8–9 of the radio and TV law (that deal with advertising) are intended to meet those reuirements, though it must be noted that in the Summer of 2025, TV 4 decided not to broadcast withland-based cable anymore (the consequences of which remain to be seen).[155] According to Chapter 9, Article 1 of the law, an obligation exists for cable and IPTV distributors to include the PBS broadcaster's (i.e., SVT) services free of charge for the consumers.

155. *See* prop 2009/10:115 p. 192 ss. – Here, it may be noted that in a survey from 2011, *Vidaresändningsplikt för tv-sändningar genom tråd*, the Media Authority (*Myndigheten för radio och TV*) stated that the current Swedish rules do meet the requirements in the Universal Services Directive. However, certain changes were suggested in Ch. 9 of the Swedish law on radio and TV, but these have not yet been enacted.

Chapter 8. Standards and Interoperability

171. Also, the so-called Universal Services Directive (2002/22) has been implemented in Swedish law, but this has been done by various measures that are sometimes difficult to trace. Article 17 of the framework directive (2002/21) on standardization is implemented by Chapter 2, Article 3 in the law on electronic communications (2003:389) and §9 in the special instruction for the Post and Tele Authority.[156] Concerning Article 18 of that directive on interoperability, there is a rule in Chapter 5, Article 12 of the law on radio and TV that deals with this in relation to disabled persons, which is seen as an implementation. It requires the highest degree of interoperability possible, while also taking the financial situation of the provider into account.[157] And according to that same law, Chapter 4, Article 9, p. 5 and Chapter 11, Article 3, p. 4, permissions to broadcast TV programmes and other radio programmes other than local or commercial ones may be given with a condition that the programmes must be made available for disabled persons. Finally, Article 24 of the directive 2002/22, juncto Annex VI, is implemented by Article 4 of the law (1998:31) and Article 2 of the regulation (1998:32) of standards for emissions of radio and TV signals. Read together, the two rules identify the radio and TV authority as responsible for enacting new rules (decrees) on all the matters mentioned in those parts of the said directive.

172. It may also be mentioned that the Government has signalled, in 2013, its wish to examine the need for further implementing measures of all the EU directives mentioned here.[158]

156. *See* http://www.pts.se.
157. A report on the situation in Sweden concerning interoperability was produced in May 2013; *see* Tillgänglighet till interoperabla televisionstjänster för personer med funktionsnedsättning, Stockholm (Stelacon/Myndigheten för radio och TV). It may also be mentioned that the latter authority decided in June 2011 to impose harsher rules on availability for disabled persons to TV programs, notably to TV 4. According to the decision, 90% of all TV must be available for all disabled persons by June 2016.
158. *See* prop 2012/13:164, Bildning och tillgänglighet – radio och TV i allmänhetens tjänst 2014–2019.

Part IV. Cross Ownership Regulation

173. When switching perspective from the issues related to freedom of speech and freedom of information, which are totally constitutionally regulated, to more specific issues of media law, which are only partly regulated by the constitutional acts described above, a few issues will immediately become clear. One such aspect is that the relation between constitutional dimensions of the law and various sorts of material law, such as competition law and intellectual property law – and thus not only criminal law and procedural law as discussed above – is here very close and clear.

174. Needless to say, all those material laws are very crucial indeed for the media sphere. One example of a recent problem related to competition law is this: Being aware of the sometimes difficult situation for Swedish newspapers, in particular the small ones, the Government has introduced, for many years, support for their production and distribution.[159] This is also the case for some cultural reviews or periodical magazines, though the Government has recently signalled its intent to reduce this. In the late 1990s, the former Social Democratic Government went one step further and initiated a legislative project aiming at reducing the dominant power of some big media companies[160] (such as the Bonnier family or the Norwegian giant A/S Schibsted, which is also a very huge actor in Sweden). This attempt, which aimed at launching a new law against so-called *media concentration* (i.e., too many media being in the hands of only a few persons or media houses), failed for various reasons, but is nevertheless interesting, since it was an ambitious attempt at studying and analysing some of the competition problems that undoubtedly exist on the Swedish media market.

175. It may be noted here that the freedom of establishment is not as such guaranteed, but rather presupposed by FPA.[161] And as mentioned above, it does in fact not exist as such (i.e., as an unconditional right) in the TV sector, which follows, at least indirectly, from the rules and somewhat complicated regulations in FSA.

176. From the competition law point of view, this has, among other aspects, also the consequence that the ordinary Swedish law on competition will probably not

159. *See* the so-called *Presstödsförordningen* (1990:524), which is administered by a special body, *Presstödsnämnden*.
160. *See* SOU 1999:30, Yttrandefriheten och konkurrensen – Förslag till mediekoncentrationslag m.m.
161. The only freedom that is expressly guaranteed by FPA is the right (for Swedish citizens) to print and then distribute: *see* Ch. 4, Art. 1 and Ch. 6, Art. 1.

apply to mergers and acquisitions within the media sector, since FPA clearly states, already in its Chapter 1, Article 1, that anyone may edit printed works (i.e., books and newspapers).[162] And since FPA is a constitutional act, it enjoys priority over ordinary legislation.[163] It may of course seem strange that national constitutional acts designed to protect freedom of speech may actually make the implementation of, e.g., EU rules intended to *strengthen* media pluralism considerably more difficult to enforce, but that is the point of departure here, anyhow. From the constitutional (FPA) point of view, a regulation whereby one buyer of a newspaper would be accepted but not another one, due to worries for media concentration or similar aspects, would simply not be acceptable, though the (constitutionally inferior) competition law contains a number of prohibitions e.g., against abuse of dominant position and cooperation between companies that may restrict free competition on a certain market.

162. *See* here also its Ch. 4, Art. 1 and Ch. 6, Art. 1, on the right to print and disseminate.
163. The committee that most recently tried to address this issue, SOU 1999:30, reluctantly (as it seems) arrived at this same conclusion; *see* in particular its Ch. 11. – As mentioned above, the rules are here slightly, but not entirely, different in the area covered by FSA. The fact that the Competition Law is based upon EU rules and supervised by a special body, *Konkurrensverket*, does not alter this, from the EU point of view, probably quite awkward situation.

Part V. Supervision: Media Regulator

177. The tasks of supervision of the various broadcasting channels have for a time been divided between the Chancellor of Justice and the above-mentioned Granskningsnämnden för radio och TV[164] (which is formally a part of Mediemyndigheten (formerly Myndigheten för radio och TV), consisting of a chairman, who shall be an active or former judge, two vice chairmen for whom the same criteria applies and six members).[165] Basically, the new authority Mediemyndigheten, director with a supervisory board of five experts,[166] is responsible for granting licences and permissions to broadcast, while the so-called Granskningsnämnden scrutinizes and supervises the programmes and the various broadcast activities that are shown or sent in Sweden.[167] Most of these decisions may be appealed to an administrative court, as described in Chapter 20 of the law. Basically, public service companies and private media operators will have to follow the same rules, but private companies – as well as the digital channel SvT Play – do not have to act impartial to quite the same extent.

164. Individual viewers may complain to this special supervisory body against programs that they do not like. Thus, in 2012, it received a total of 1.189 complaints against different radio and TV programs, a figure that was slightly lower than the previous years. Programs may be criticized for lack of objectivity or impartiality, for violations of privacy, depiction of violence or pornography, for being too commercial or favouring certain products and on some other, similar grounds. Sanctions are normally economical, maybe also in combination with an obligation to inform about the decision made against the company.

165. All of whom are appointed by the Government, as follows at least indirectly from Ch. 16, Art. 14 of the Radio and TV law. – In December 2013, this authority (*Myndigheten för radio och TV*) was asked by the Government to examine how the existence of public service TV and radio channels, that still hold a prominent place in the broadcasting area, does affect the media market as a whole. (Ministry of Culture, 19 Dec. 2013, decision no. Ku2013/2522/MFI). The decision to conduct such a survey may be seen as partly ideological, since the former, right-wing government was more positive towards private operators in the media market than the previous or current one. –This seems to be in line with a communication on public service issued by the EU Commission in 2009 (IP/09/1072). As mentioned above, the government issued a new bill on public service in June 2013 (prop 2012/13:164, Bildning och tillgänglighet – radio och TV i allmänhetens tjänst 2014–2019), where, among other things, digitalization of the whole radio network as of 2022 was proposed (though later delayed,as mentioned above).

166. For further details, *see* the regulation 2010:1062.

167. For details, *see* Ch. 16 of the law.

Selected Bibliography

Laws

Tryckfrihetsförordningen (1949:105), *Freedom of Press Act* and Yttrandefrihetsgrundlagen (1991:1469), *Freedom of Speech Act*, are two of Sweden's four Constitutional Acts. Regeringsformen, (1974:152), *Instrument of Government*, is the main Constitution.

Lag (1991:1559) med föreskrifter på tryckfrihetsförordningens och yttrandefrihetsgrundlagens områden.

Konkurrenslagen (2008:604), *Competition law.*

Marknadsföringslagen (2008:486), *Marketing Law.*

Offentlighets- och Sekretesslagen, (2009:400).

Radio- och TV-lagen (2010:696).

Selected Bibliography

List of Cases

Swedish Supreme Court (Högsta Domstolen):
NJA 1973 p. 423
NJA 1975 p. 589
NJA 1977 p. 751
NJA 1988 p. 572
NJA 1989 p. 131
NJA 1990 p. 636
NJA 1991 p. 512
NJA 1998 p. 817
NJA 1998 p. 848
NJA 1999 p. 275
NJA 2001 p. 409
NJA 2001 p. 445
NJA 2005 p. 805
NJA 2005 p. 884
NJA 2012 p. 342
NJA 2012 p. 400
NJA 2014 p. 94
NJA 2015 p. 298
NJA 2024 p. 618
NJA 2025 p. 123
Swedish Supreme Administrative Court (Högsta Förvaltningsdomstolen, before 2011 Regeringsrätten):
RÅ 1974 p. 121
RÅ 1990 ref. 75
RÅ 1995 ref. 58
RÅ 1997 ref. 65
RÅ 2010 p. 115 (I–II)
HFD 2014 ref. 33
HFD 2024 ref. 43
Uppsala City Court:
Judgment of 23 December 2013, Case T 1958-12
Court of Appeal, Stockholm (Svea Hovrätt):
Judgment of 26 November 2014, T 803-14
Marknadsdomstolen (Swedish Market Court):
MDA 2003:5

List of Cases

European Court of Justice

C-288/89, *Stichting Collectieve Antennevoorziening Gouda*, ECR 1991 I p. 4007.
C-368/95, *Familiapress*, ECR 1997 I p. 3689.
C-405/98, *Gourmet*, ECR 2001 I p. 1795.
C-101/01, *Lindquist*, ECR 2003 I p. 12971.
C-71/02, *Karner*, ECR 2004 I p. 3025.
C-380/03, *Germany v. Parliament and Council*, ECR 2006 I p. 11573.
C-185/09, *Commission v. Sweden,* Judgment 4 February 2010, ECR 2010 I p. 14.
C-283/11, *Sky Österreich GmbH*, ECR 2013:28 Joined Cases C-293/12, *Digital Rights Ireland* and C-594/12, Seitlinger and Others, Judgment 8 April 2014
C-698/15, Tele2, EU:C:2016:970C-311/18, 'Schrems Facebook', EU:C:2020:559
C-231/12, *Google Spain,* EU:C:2014:317
European Court of Human Rights:
Holm v. Sweden, Judgment 25 November 1993, Series No. 279 – A.
Bladet Tromsö and Stensaas v. Norway, 21980/93, Judgment 20 May 1999, ECHR 1999-III, Hudoc ref. 1216.
VGT v. Switzerland, Appl. no. 24699/94, Judgment 28 June 2001.
Caroline von Hannover v. Germany, Judgment 24 June 2004, 59320/00.

Literature

Axberger, Hans-Gunnar: Yttrandefrihetsgrundlagarna, Stockholm (Norstedts Juridik) 2012.

Funcke, Nils: Tryckfriheten – Ordets män och statsmakterna, Stockholm 2006.

Galtung, Andreas (red.), Medierätten – nya utvecklingslinjer, Nordisk Årsbok i Rättsinformatik 1995, Stockholm (Norstedts Juridik) 1995.

Justitiekanslern 300 år, Uppsala (Iustus) 2013.

Lundell, Bengt/Strömberg, Håkan: Grundlagsskyddad yttrandefrihet, 15th ed, Lund (Studentlitteratur) 2013.

Medieutveckling 2013, Myndigheten för radio och TV, Stockholm 2013 (available at http://mediemyndigheten.se).

Nergelius, Joakim: Svensk statsrätt, 5th ed, Lund (Studentlitteratur) 2022.

Constitutional Reform in Sweden. Some important remarks, Tijdschrift voor Constitutioneel Recht (Netherlands) 2013 pp. 372–379.

Olsson, Anders R.: Yttrandefrihet & Tryckfrihet – Handbok för journalister, Lund (Studentlitteratur) 2012.

Persson, Gunnar: Exklusivitetsfrågan: Om förhållandet mellan tryckfrihet, yttrandefrihet och annan rätt, Stockholm 2002.

Ruotsi, Mikael: Svensk yttrandefrihet och internationell rätt – Det grundlagsskyddade tryck- och yttrandefriheten och dess relation till Europakonventionen, EU-rätten och FN:s konvention om medborgerliga och politiska rättigheter, Uppsala 2020.

Schmauch, Magnus: Tio år av besynnerligheter – artikel 4.2 FEU och konstitutionell identitet, Svensk Juristtidning 2025 pp. 634–656.

The Constitution of Sweden – The Fundamental Laws and the Riksdag Act, Sveriges Riksdag, Stockholm 2012.

Tillgänglighet till interoperabla televisionstjänster för personer med funktionsnedsättning, Stockholm 2013 (Stelacon/Myndigheten för radio och TV).
Vallinder, Torbjörn: Nio edsvurna män – Jury och tryckfrihet i Sverige 1815–2000, Stockholm 2000.
Warnling-Nerep, Wiweka & Bernitz, Hedvig: En orientering i tryckfrihet & yttrandefrihet, 5th ed., Stockholm (Jure) 2013.
World Press Freedom Index 2024 – Reporters Without Borders (Reportrar utan gränser, https://reportrarutangranser.se) 2024.

Index

The numbers here refer to paragraph numbers.

Index

www.ingramcontent.com/pod-product-compliance
Lightning Source LLC
Chambersburg PA
CBHW071357230926
51846CB00002B/576

9789403568102